OFF-LEASH HUMOUR

By

Cornelius N. Eneh

Copyright 2018 by Nwachukwu Cornelius Eneh

CONTENTS

INTRODUCTION 1
CHAPTER ONE 2
CHAPTER TWO 8
CHAPTER THREE 16
CHAPTER FOUR 22
CHAPTER FIVE 34
CHAPTER SIX 40
CHAPTER SEVEN 49
CHAPTER EIGHT 75
CHAPTER NINE 83
CHAPTER TEN 89
CHAPTER ELEVEN 97
CHAPTER TWELVE 111

INTRODUCTION

Humans possess the inherent ability to reason, act and to communicate their thoughts to fellow humans. Sometimes the ability to communicate effectively become hindered by language barriers, but we can still take good advantage of the reasoning and acting ability to convey our thoughts and ideas. Just like the humans, animals are also equipped to reason and act but are limited in their ability to vocalize their thoughts in a way that humans can understand. Hence the communication links between animals and their human counterparts are short-chained. Nevertheless, it cannot be ruled out totally that within the different species of animals, each species can reason, act and communicate thoughts and ideas among themselves in different languages and signs not understood by humans. On interactive levels, dogs rank the highest and closest to humans when compared with other species of animals in their ability to communicate ideas, thoughts, actions and reactions to situations. If only humans care to know.

CHAPTER ONE

I LOVE IT when the park is warm; more so with nice, clear weather and full of users as it is today. As the sun makes its glorious descent, it is filtering

in rays of light along the few pathways that are not covered by the vast expanse of the tree canopies. Days are gone when the sun rays were in full monopoly of the majority of the park. In those days, park users are in closer proximity to one another as they huddled together under the few young trees that offer partial coverage from the sun, hot at this time of the year. Many of us then, do not accompany their families to the park for fear of confrontations. We were always at, unprovoked war with one another whenever and wherever we meet, for no obvious reasons. No wonder the humans always kept us apart. Humans tied us to the tree trunk with metal chain leash in an effort to make it possible for the different families to enjoy peaceful co-existence without any botheration from us. I like the humans and envy their freedom. Things have changed a lot for the better since then. However, it did not happen over-night. This park has been extended far beyond what it used to be in those days. The growth of these trees in size and number intrigues me the most. The same is the case with the wide variety of wild birds, squirrels, bunnies not to mention the different kinds of insects, as well as dogs like me in this park. These different species communicate in their respective terms and signs, each minding their own business. But once in a while it is not unusual to observe one of us chasing squirrels and rodents for no reason at all.

Oh, good to mention, we come in different shapes, sizes, forms and above all, with varying attitudes.

Look at that busy body Jackie over there. She is not as big as my head alone for sure, but too active for her size. Would she give peace to these poor little rodents and allow them access to the left over, crumbs of bread inside the waste bin? Never! But I am sure she is well fed by her owner. If not, after chasing them away, why would she simply walks away not wanting the wastes? Little wonder humans refer to us as being in the manger.

Wait a minute, did I just say owner? I was never owned by Mr. Jones. I am more like a son he never had and he treated me as such. Sometimes I imagine that this little monster is, somehow rewarded by the park overseers to direct and control these poor creatures struggling to ward off starvation. By right, they should not starve while the humans are wasting precious food.

Talk about forms, there she comes as huge as I am.

With all those hairs over her face, how does she make her way through objects in her home and here in the park without stumbling upon things? May be, she simply lumps herself down like I do, day dreaming and wondering over things that do not concern me. That comes with age I believe. I wasn't like this when I was younger. Without any noticeable hairs on my body sometimes the heat of the day drives me insane. I can only imagine what she is going through at this season of the year. But I am sure she must feel very comfortable during the colder months. She is no doubt a gentle giant. I hate those months especially, as much as I miss being in the park. What a funny sight! That one is like a log of wood. I am sure she has legs but looks like she is crawling on her belly.

Just like me, she has no hairs on her body. It will be fun to  watch her completely covered by the snow when she is out to do her thing outside in winter, since her legs, I am sure are just slightly longer than the longest toes on my feet. Luckily, her ears are droopy enough to prevent snow entering her ear canal. While outside in the snow all you will likely notice above the snow is the tip of her tail which is always held upright and the tip of her nose to let in the cold air.

 Unfortunately, that funny site would last for a twinkle of eyes, otherwise she will freeze into a solid mass buried in the snow. It interests me to sit by this

bench and watch the different species communicate, in their own terms and signs and minding their own business. A few days ago, and right across from my spot here, one of us I believe, was taken out of a lady's hand bag.

At first I could not believe what I observed.

I cast out a curious attention towards him. I wondered whether the humans really think he and I belong to the same species. He is just about half the size of my head. Being tossed away into a lady's hand bag is quite unfair. I was sure he hated me for my curiosity. I could notice his eyes almost popped out of its socket in disbelief at seeing me too. He started barking ferociously and quickly lunched at me only to be restrained by the lady who yelled at him "stop it Chiw and behave better. Can you fight him? He can swallow us up without chewing the bones." But in my opinion she should have dignified him better by not putting him inside that hand bag and bringing him out to the public. His continuous barking really scared me and forced me to leave the park earlier than usually. As I was leaving I wondered within me what he would have done to me if he was not restrained from attacking me? Or rather, how would I have reacted in order to protect myself from his potential arsenal? May be, I would have been stunned with mouth wide open, only to feel him dive in right down my throat without realising it, and probably without causing much damage in the process. Again, I am drifting away in my thoughts. May be, it is better to take a walk and do my business. Oh, no! Why is he on my bench now? I just left the spot a little while ago or did I wander away too long not realising it? Definitely he must be up to some mischief and I am not ready for his trouble. Good bye little one. The spot is all yours today. I'm gone and let you be the winner. Why invite trouble for myself. Home is always safer, Mr. Jones usually said.

CHAPTER TWO

I OBSERVE THAT MORE and more families are now using the park, under the canopy of trees, among other things to escape the heat of summer. The difference this time is that interaction between families have declined considerably as each family forms an island of its own in complete exclusion of the others. When they do interact, it is usually to celebrate special occasions. Let me not forget to mention the landscaping now, which is highly maintained with lush green lawn. I have seen so many friends over the years, some of which I had bitter confrontations during my earlier days in this park, for reasons I cannot explain now. I was very young then. Things have really changed in this park, among the users. All I do these days is just sit here and marvel at the changes. The most remarkable of the changes being that none of us is tied to a leash here, any longer. All, are free to run around without restrictions and confrontations. At worst, we sniff each other's behind, make gestures, part ways or become play mates. But the sniffing thing is what I do not understand. I do not sniff and hate being sniffed. The little ones are into it and I do not understand why they do that.

One in particular makes it a point to sniff all in the park before he leaves.

I wonder if it has anything to do with the flatness of his face which has turned much darker than any other part of his body. Nose sunken and eyeballs almost off the socket due to constant exposure to poops, I believe. She is always on the move, bold and full of self-confidence. She will approach anyone, big or small, without fear or hesitation, sniffs and walks away. She has no time for socialisation and any kind of intimidation is challenged to the fullest extent. I take interest just watching her sniffing around. Though small, I look upon her as many of us rolled into one body. Everything said and done, I am confident that a day will come when we will all move around freely in all the other parks, like the humans, unleashed to and in the park. All it takes is for us to love and tolerate each other. How and when that will happen is everybody's guess. Although these days, I do not have the strength, to run around catching freebies and teasing the squirrels, I still enjoy being in my own world, navigating my thoughts from the memories of the past to the present-day realities. I am glad that I lived long enough to witness the transitions that have taken place in this park. Nothing would have pleased Mr. Jones better if he had lived a bit longer. This park meant everything for him when he was alive.

Growing up in this neighbourhood was remarkable giving that Mr. Jones raised me with so much care and love that I was almost turned into a spoilt brat. He was very protective and would never let go of me an inch. He would ride me to this park in a baby pram ignoring curious gazes and ugly comments from park users. What! A puppy in a baby pram? Who is he and what is he up to?" He was least bothered by those ugly comments. At this very park bench he would seat me by his side and reads from his "Evening Times" newspaper until I fall asleep resting my head on his lap. This very tree was the specially chosen by Mr. Jones because it was the tallest of the trees in the part providing, just adequate shade for the two of us. Moreover, the spot is located by the corner, just at the entrance to the park. That meant least interaction with the other dogs and no chaining to a tree. Mr.

Jones was very particular about that fact. "No leash on my Blonn, no, never!" he would insist. We were always among the first user to enter the park and occupy our spot which later was popularly termed Mr.

Jones' bench". No one dares occupy Mr. Jones' bench even on the few days that we did not visit the park.

"Hey there, did you see my freebee? It flew past where you are seated now into that bush behind you.

I need it right away. Can you be of any help? I am sure you must have seen it fly pass you. You better sit up please and help locate it instead of idling away like bundle of what I don't know. As you can see, I am extremely very busy right now and have little or no time to waste. What's wrong with you? Don't tell me that you have no idea of what I am searching for because you should have seen the bright red freebee whistle pass right above your head, into the small bush just behind you unless you were dozing away. Ah, there it is. I have found it. Bye grandpa."

Dear me! That's a hot number. How does that brat expect me to watch over his freebee? Does he even realise that I cannot see clearly objects just beyond the tip of my nose? All I know is that he is really enjoying his youth. Kind of youthful exuberance. But still I admire his boldness, freedom of expression and agility. I am sure I will find him funny and interesting to deal with. Come to think of it, at his age I would have liked to enjoy the freedom to express myself without fears. Mr. Jones never allowed a little bit of room for me to be myself and explore my surroundings. But instead he was more interested to protect me from harm. I was always too big for my age at any stage compared to those of us around in the park. I was sure none would dare intimidate me then. But still Mr. Jones knew better because in the dog world, size is not always a deterrent to bad hostile behaviours. Here comes my friend and I wonder what he is in pursuit of this time. I did not see any freebee flying over me at the moment.

"I am very tired. Mind if I sit beside you, grandpa? I am exhausted running around with my playmates. Very good friends, you know. Did you ever enjoy the company of good friends before you became old? I mean running around, throwing and catching whatever you called it then. I run faster than all my playmates, you know."

"You are welcome to sit beside me. I admire your youth which I wasn't lucky to experience when I was your age. Where is your family?"

"My family is down there by the lake."

"Don't tell me that you ran all the way up here by yourself. Your family must be looking for you."

"No, grandpa, they will not. I am always on my own as usual in this park running around, throwing and catching freebee with my play mates. I only regroup with my family when it is time to go home."

"Your playmates allow you to join them without attacking you. I am surprised to hear that. I always think that playing together is out of the way when you meet for the very first time."

"No, why, we don't behave that way here in this park. Outside the park, yes but here no. Fun, isn't it?"

"Eh, it is but… eh. Ok, never mind. You may still call me grandpa. I don't mind that but my name is Blonn. Blonn Jones.

"Blonn? What kind of name is that and who gave it to you? These humans are really strange to me especially our owners. I rather call you grandpa if you don't mind me doing so.

"The choice is entirely yours, but I go by the name Blonn. The name given to me by my father, Mr. Jones. He was not my "owner." He was my father and always referred to me as sonny meaning "my son." By the way, what is your name sonny?"

"That's why humans are strange to me, very hard to believe in them. Grandpa do you believe all that the humans tell us. They tell us one thing today and do something else moments later. Still we adore and believe in them to the very last breath in us. But do you call him father or dad as well?"

"I never called him by any name because there was no need for me to do so. Just by looking up at him he understood my needs and solves it far beyond my expectations." So, what's your name sonny and who is your …?"

"Eh grandpa, Sonny is not my name, but at the same time, I would like to see what Mr. Jones is or looks like. He sounds to me different from what humans appear to be"

"I wish I could bring him to you but…"

"But what? You claimed he is a nice man. What are you throwing at me to force me to change my opinion about humans?"

"He was but he is no…"

"No, what? There you are. I hope he did not check you out of his life at this stage of your old…"

"No he did not do what you are thinking and I hate to assume that all humans are unreliable. Almost all those Mr. Jones interacted with were as nice as he was."

"That's the reason I am desperate to meet him. Is that also too hard for you to do? Oh, no, this old age is a disaster as I can see now. Do I really want to grow old judging from all that I see and hear? The answer is no."

"Ok, if you would be patient enough to allow me finish my sentence before your interruption, let me say that Mr. Jones is no more, and by that, I mean that he is dead. I would do anything to bring him…wait a minute, is it that really difficult to pull out a definite answer from you. Once again, what is your name? Don't tell me you don't have a name."

"Grandpa, my owner is here now. Unfortunately, I have to leave now. May be, I would like to talk with you here again tomorrow. Bye grandpa"

"Bye sonny, come to me whenever you can. Nice, knowing you".

What a brat! Did I manage to outwit him or was he really that smart or hard to take on? All the same, I am developing a soft corner for him in my heart and I am beginning to like his witty nature. May be, I need to learn to be and act in the present. But at this age what more can I learn to outsmart the young. Something to think about. A kind of food for thought. It is getting late now. I have to go home. What a day!"

CHAPTER THREE

I DON'T THINK "sonny" or whatever his name could be, is in the park today. I really miss him not minding his witty nature. Mrs. Jones illness is playing on my mind. Her care person thinks that everything will be alright. For a couple of days now she did not accompany me to the park and I miss her too. She will be ok am sure.

Is that not my sonny? He is in a very high spirit dashing at that speed into the park to meet his play mates. I don't blame him but I hope he remembers to say hi to grandpa.

What a gorgeous one! I remember seeing her sometime back in full hair. If I remember correctly, her owner calls her Pooly and she is equally gorgeous. They complement each other very well. What a nice job done to her hair. With her hairs sculptured in balls around the ankles, elbows, hip region, chest, on top of her head and tip of her tail. No doubt she has all the patience in the world to withstand whatever it takes to get the job done on her. I wonder what I would look like if I had long hairson my body. I heard it is not fun to get groomed if the hairs are that long. With all the tugging, pulling the hairs to detangle, followed by washing, drying, blow drying hair, they say is very noisy and stressful, followed by trimming the hair. I would go insane by the time it is over for me. As I am now, it takes me little or no time to wash and dry up my skin. No hair to worry about. I must ask Sonny how he feels to be groomed. He has long hairs but I don't think he gets groomed like her. As little and hyper active as he is, I wonder how one can groom him. My eyes are beginning to close. I think I need a short nap. Gentle breeze like this usually lures me to sleep and unless I nap now I would be cranky all the way for the rest of the day.

"Eh, eh!"

"Hey! Who!! Who!!! Oh, sonny it's you. I must have dozed off. I smacked myself really hard on the cheek. I am always afraid of spider, tiny insects and flies entering my ears. Where, are you coming from?"

"Ha!Ha!Ha! Grandpa, I think I frightened you. I could hear you snoring from a distance. So, I thought that the best way to wake you up will be to tickle your long ears. So, I plucked this dried grass blade, gently lifted your ear. You did not move, tugged on it gently, then harder, harder and still harder but nothing happened. You came to life only when I shoved the blade into the canal. Do you really sleep that deep? I could have lifted you up and out of the park without you realising what was happening to you. Those ears are really big. Very funny to see you startled that much. Why do you need such long ear lobes? I am sure you do not know how loud your snoring is and how far the sound that you make travels. Those long ear lobes of yours are to blame. Better get your hearing checked but don't go to that... eh I forgot what they call him. I am referring to the one right across from this park. First thing he does as soon as you entered place, is to probe anus with a glass stick, lift it up right above his nose, to smell it I believe, murmur a few words to your owner. Before you know what's going on he sticks a needle into your bum. It pains a lot, grandpa and I still don't understand why he does that to me and everyone who steps into his trap, I'm sure. That's why I don't like him."

"Are you referring to the vet? Sonny, you are very funny. Your ears are not as long as mine I know. I am sure that you snore just like everyone else. But you will not realise that now, until you become old and tired. Glad to see you today. Next time try lifting me up but I am afraid I might fall over and flatten you to the ground in the process. Do you know what that means? Sure, you do, sonny."

"I don't think I want to get old. Lying idle all the time, losing my vision, hearing hard and snoring very loud for all to hear.

Not for me. Grandpa, how old are you and did you ever run around fast like me in the park? When I grow as big as you are, I will continue to run even faster. I admire your ear lobes. When mine grow that long I would like to flap it across my face to dispel foul smell. Do you do that sometimes, grandpa?"

"Sonny, you will grow older than I am now but you will never grow as big as I am. You might as well forget the hope of growing your ear lobes much longer than it is now because that will never happen. As for my age, let me put it this way. You see, sonny, when I was your age most of these trees in this park were much smaller than they are now. And some of them were not even there. The grasses were not everywhere as they are now. And ..."

"Grandpa, are you sure of what you are telling me. Sometimes we imagine and forget things at old age. That's why I do not want to grow old. I want to remain as I am for ever."

"Sonny, that is not how it happens. You have to grow old someday. It was not possible for me to run around in this park when I was your age."

"Why not grandpa?"

"We were not allowed to do so, in those days. Some of us were always chained to the trees but Mr. Jones never tied me to the tree. He always kept me seated by him with my head resting on his leg."

"But why were dogs like me chained to the tree instead of being free to run around? That's cruel, to me. Don't you think so? Wish I could trust humans better. When are, you going to take me to Mr. Jones grandpa?"

"Like I said, sonny, in those days, we fight among ourselves all the time for no reason at all whenever we were brought together. The humans did not like that behaviour at all. The only way, for them to maintain peace in the park then was to bring us on leash and tie us to the trees. But I was never tied to a tree. Mr. Jones will never allow that."

"I have heard so much about Mr. Jones, grandpa. Are you or are you not going to take me to meet him? That's not fair. I am eager to meet a reasonable human and from your account he appears to be the only one alive."

"Sonny, I will never take you to him. You have to be dead to meet him and I don't wish you dead."

"But you said he is a good man, why do I have to be dead to meet him, grandpa?"

"He was a good man, but now he is dead and gone. We will never be able to see him again. You see sonny, I will never take you to him. Do you understand now?"

"Yes, I do. You should have told me long ago that Mr. Jones was dead."

"I tried to, but you were not patient to listen to what I was trying to explain to you. In the mean, time your owner came and you had to leave."

Sorry, grandpa. Are you getting to cry? Your droopy eyes are getting filled up with tears but at your age you should never cry. Only the small babies cry all around. And you are not a baby. There comes my owner. I may see you tomorrow and shall get something for you. Don't cry grandpa, bye."

"Bye sonny. You are so encouraging. I promise you, grandpa will not cry and thank you for your concern."

CHAPTER FOUR

I LEFT THE PARK YESTERDAY with mixed feelings. I have never felt so emotional about Mr. Jones since he died long ago, the way I felt talking to sonny. I could not believe how he was able to detect the tears welling in my eyes before a drop strolled down my cheek. I hope that I did not upset him. He is hyperactive but at the same time very loving and compassionate. His promise to get something for me today really moved my spirit. He simply did not want me to remain depressed remembering and thinking about Mr. Jones. It lightened my mood before I reached home to Mrs. Jones. She, on the other had a good news from her healthcare giver. She will live much longer than we anticipated. That's all I wanted to hear. These couple of days I spent alone in the park without her were painful. I preferred to be by her side all the time but she always insisted on me spending sometime in usual way, in the park. "The fresh air and the company of the other park users will be good to your health" she always said. But it is never the same when she is not there with me. Tugging on her wheelchair to and from the park brings a lot of memories of me being strolled to the park in a baby stroller. Mr. Jones was all alone then so I was everything to him. When he became very ill a healthcare giver was employed to attend to him on certain days. She was very caring to both of us and calls me sonny too. Later she became Mrs. Jones. Everything went well in the house for a long, long time. It was all joy and laughter in the house and I never saw Mr. Jones so happy in life. The two of us were the only things he cared for in life. One faithful day, as Mr. Jones' illness took a turn for the worse, he had a long conversation with Mrs. Jones while he was still lying in bed. At the end of it all I was informed that he was not in a position to sit in the park because of his condition. She strolled me down to the park, sat down on our usual bench and she said to me:

"Sonny, right now only the two of us are left in our house. Mr. Jones, I am afraid may not be with us much longer. His doctor said he has only a few hours left to live. His heart will stop breathing any moment from now. The health authorities are on their way to take him to where he will spend the rest of his life. There he will be taken better care of in a very special way until he dies. He will not see us again. He loved you so much that he cannot stand the sight of tears on your cheeks.

"Mrs. Jones, do you say that I will not see my daddy again. If we go back to the house now I can still …"

"No sonny, it is late. He has been taken away soon after we left the house. He promised me that he will always love you wherever he might be. He told me to call you by your name "Bonn" because you are "son" only to Mr. Jones and no other. He also made me promise him that we will take care of each other to the very end. I gave him my word that Blonn would be taken good care of and I am sure you will take care of me as well."

That faithful day will always remain a nightmare to me. The thought of reaching home any day and not meeting Mrs. Jones still haunts me. It was a big relief to know that she will be ok and will lead a long life. I don't know what I would do without Mrs. Jones. I am hoping that soon she will be well enough to come to the park with me. I miss her a lot.

"Hey! Sonny what happened to you now. You look so sad and worried. What happened to you today. I am sure you have not met your playmates yet. Why? Come on puppy,

tell grandpa Blonn. I will make sure that I stand up for you."

"Grandpa, can you just come with me and take away Princess.

Take her away and never allow her to return to Mr. Smith's house anymore. She is very irritating, annoying and likes to dominate Budo and I all the time. Mr. Smith will always take up for her. Once she is gone I can handle Budo, that fat lump."

"Wow, wow! Wait a minute sonny, who is Princess and who is Budo? Mr. Smith no doubt, is your owner if, I must call him that."

"Grandpa, Princess thinks that she is in charge of all of us. She is over pampered by Mr. Smith. She has a special perch high up on a table where she climbs up and look down on Budo and I. She knows we cannot climb."

Budo is a fat lump and so very indifferent. He has no interest in what is happening around him. He bothers no one as long as he is not hungry. He also comes with us to the park, but plays with no one. He is too fat to run. All he does in the park is to lump himself down in a corner, lost in his own world and fart. Whenever he is hungry he wonders around looking for something to eat. I always cautioned him that one day he

will chew down the liter materials in Princess' poop box which look like our dry food. He wouldn't mind that happening, so long as it fills his tummy."

"Ok, now what did Princess do to you that is making you so angry with her?"

"You know, Budo and I are usually taken out to do our business. You know what I mean, and Mr. Smith picks after us. Grandpa, may I ask who picks after you? Huge pile up for sure. That must be a big deal. I am always fascinated to see the amount of deal that Budo voids each time we were taken out. I cannot describe to you how much it stinks. He is of course much smaller than you in size. But Princess does not have to go out to do her business. But instead Mr. Smith provided for her a special tote filled with litter material which she uses. Very close to my bed but I must admit that she knows how to cover up her poop and pee after using the tote. You hardly see anything left above the litter materials. Very secretive. So, poor Mr. Smith picks after us and scoops after her."

"Lucky Princess! If Mr. Smith takes good care the three of you in special ways, without complaining, then what is your problem sonny?"

"Not that grandpa, I could not sleep on my bed last night."

"Why not, sonny?"

"Because Princess did her business on my bed, before I got home from the park the other day, grandpa. That was the reason I did not accompany Mr. Smith and our neighbours to the park yesterday."

"What did you do then and how are you sure she did it and not Budo?"

"Grandpa, I know the difference between the huge dump from Budo and what will come out of her even though she does good job of covering it with her liter materials. She did not attempt to cover it. Little bits of the materials were there on my bed. As soon as she saw me enter the house she skipped onto her high perch table and steadied her mischievous gaze on me. Very mischievous little brat. I hated her for being so disrespectful and up to many unpredictable silly things. That was not the first time she did it on my bed."

"Has she ever tried that mischief on Budo's bed before? If not, maybe he is nicer to her"?

"No, grandpa, Budo never steps out of his bed. All he does is sleep, eat, poop and sleep again. That's why he is very fat. You must hear him grunting on the way to do his business. And he loves to sleep. Sometimes he is so engrossed in his sleep that he lies on his back snoring, with head tilted to one side and his four legs pointing to the ceiling. That is who Budo is. If you take Princess away, so far that she would not be able to trace her way back to Mr. Smith, I can handle Budo easily. I just have to guard my food and make sure he does not steal it. Budo and I have been very comfortable with each other until Mr. Smith brought Princess. At first we thought she was a boarder to be picked up after a couple of days, by the lady who brought her to us. But, that didn't happen so she stayed on. Grandpa that's why I think you and I should plan to take her away to somewhere else. She does not belong to our house. Budo and I will never be happy with her around"

"Ok! Sonny, how do you get along with Budo? Does he bother you in any way?

"You know grandpa, when Mr. Smith brought Budo home as a little puppy, I had similar problem with him. He was always in a playful mood. I would play with him as much as I can but when he over does it I simply snare at him to express my displeasure."

"And what will he do?"

"He gets scared of me. Poor thing, he will simply submit, falls to the ground on his back with his legs up. Unlike Princess, he cannot climb any height and he so cannot escape me. That was then, but now he is much bigger than I am. He scares me sometimes. Now I remember, he pees everywhere and that annoys both Mr. Smith and I. As time goes on he became house trained and behaved better. As a puppy, he loved to eat. He would finish his feed and want mine as well."

"How did you handle that, sonny?"

"It took a while for me to break that bad habit of his, and this is how I did it. First, Mr. Smith will serve us feed on separate dishes. I will stand by my bowl and watch him gobble down his. Next, he would move toward mine. I will snare at him displaying all the teeth in my mouth. The look on my face would convince him that I was capable of swallowing him along with the feed in his tummy. With that he backs away but still maintain a steady gaze on my bowl of feed. Right now, I can leave my bowl full of feed and walk away. He keeps staring at it but will not attempt to steal it. Grandpa don't you think I trained him properly? Another bad behaviour he developed as he grew older was jumping and humping on things all the time. I was disgusted with that attitude and so was Mr. Smith who kept yelling stop, Budo Stop! But do you think he will listen. One day Mr. Smith took him to that... do you call him vet? See the vet and when they returned Budo changed and behaved better. The vet really taught Budo a good lesson.

"Oh no, Sonny he got snipped. The vet snipped him. I know that for sure"

"Grandpa, I don't know what you are talking about but all I know is that all of a sudden, Budo learned to behave better, no longer jumps and humps, but his appetite grew more and he started putting on weight so much that now he finds it difficult to move around especially when his feed bowl is empty. Eh! grandpa, did that vet thought you the same lesson that made you eat more and become too fat like you are now?"

"Maybe you are right, sonny. I am sure Budo got snipped by that vet. And I am sure you got snipped as well. Yes, you are, even though you did and may never become fat like Budo and I."

"Grandpa, I never liked that vet especially when he picks up that syringe and the needle and approaches me. I cannot remember him teaching the lesson that he taught Budo and that's why I am not fat like the two of you. But grandpa why don't you try to eat less? When you eat less you poop less and become less fat so that you can run around fast like me"

"Sonny, you did an excellent job of him, but don't you think that if you tried harder you will equally train Princess to behave better? All you have to do is to give her a chance to change with time"

"Grandpa, believe me she will never change for better and not with that height advantage using the cat perch. I wish we are capable of climbing heights as well. Oh! You know what happened the other day? A squirrel strayed into the house to steal some feed from feed storage bin kept on the table. That happens from time to time. The, poor little creature was just long enough to grab a couple of pellets when it was spotted by Princess the big boss. It dashed for an escape but not fast enough to escape from Princess who pinned it down with those sharp toe nails of hers. But before she could cause more harm, the squirrel caught hold of her tail and bit her so hard that she let go of it with a scary scream. Budo and I watched the whole episode from the floor I found it very entertaining. Princess nursed that wound for a long time. Mr. Smith took her regularly to the vet, that wicked, ok, never mind. The look, on her face revealed not a pleasure trip at all. Since that day, at the least opportunity, the squirrel along with the relatives and siblings, I believe, come over on self-invitation, feast around the feed bin whenever Mr. Smith is not in the house. What I enjoy the most is watching Princess gazing at the feasting guests helplessly. She learned her lesson in a bitter way.

"Sonny I guess you are having busy time at home with so many different activities going on. For me I have only Mrs. Jones at home and these days she is not keeping too well. Lucky for us, her health care giver had good news for us. She is getting better and will lead a long life. That means she will be accompanying me to this park soon, as usual. I am glad she is getting better. Don't worry sonny, you will be fine."

"What fine, grandpa? Take that Princess and give her away to some home where she belongs. I am sure she will be scared to see you and she deserves to be. I always told Mr. Smith to send her back to that lady or to the place where a less fortunate home will adopt her. But he always says "give her a chance, Carl. She will definitely behave better and learn to adjust with all of us".

"Sonny, that's exactly what I am suggesting to you. Mr. Smith understands behaviours better. Try to give Princess a chance to learn to adjust with you. She will surprise you some day, I am sure."

"No grandpa, I don't think she will ever change but Mr. Jones will never agree with me. You will not believe what mischief she does in the house. Mr. Smith always takes up for her. He bought that perch table for her and I don't see the reason or the need for that. It gives the height advantage over Budo and I. Once up there she looks down on us as though she is the boss to supervisor us and we are her servants. That is what frustrates me about Princess. I am fed-up."

Wow, Wow, Wow! Hold on a minute sonny. Looks like you have another one in your home. Really busy place I must admit. Now, who is that Carl you just mentioned about? Good or bad to you? Tell me more about Carl."

"Grandpa, looks like you are back to your day dreaming world again. How many times must I tell you that Mr. Smith calls me Carl. Have you forgotten? That's why I do not want to get old. I don't want to keep forgetting things right after I heard it. Have you had your ears checked recently by the vet recently? That's another wicked one I do not want to recall. And grandpa, for the third time added to one, Mr. Smith calls me Carl, and don't forget again. You can still call me sonny if you choose to, but my name is Carl, Carl Smith. Just call me Carl. Very easy to remember, grandpa."!!!!!!!!!!!!

"Carl! That's a sweet name you know, even though it took forever, for that name to drop off your lip like a thunder bolt. I like that name and I shall always call you by Carl. But I am still grandpa, remember"

"I have to go now and if Princess acts funny with me again something has to be done, grandpa. We will plan and send her to a rescue center, you and I. Whether Mr. Smith likes it or not she better behaves herself or she will be gone for good. I pity the next home she finds herself in. Goodbye and try to come up with a plan tomorrow."

"Goodbye Carl. Don't worry, you will be fine".

CHAPTER FIVE

POOR THING! I CAN feel his frustration. I am glad Mr. and Mrs. Jones do not like cats. They always maintained that we are by far more friendly compared to cats. According to them cats are too bold for their liking and less affectionate. They come to you when they are in need some attention. And how do they achieve that? By sliding and rubbing their trunk and tail continually between your legs, in the process. And once they achieved their goal they are gone. turn their back on you, easily. Other points against cats are their defensive tendency and their readiness to fight back at any cost without submission. But how can I convince Carl that cats, though small, are never a walk over. He has to see with Mr. Smith and give Princess a chance to change. I know he wouldn't welcome that idea readily and no matter how I tried to persuade him in this line he would always play the ball back to me in a teasing way. He is good at that I must admit. But I have to give it a shot. I hate to see him frustrated in any form.

"Grandpa come, walk up here fast. I have something interesting to tell you."

"Hey! Carl, you appear very happy and excited today, what happened?"

"Just walk faster grandpa and hear me out. What's wrong with your legs? They don't seem to be happy under your trunk. I won't blame them for feeling the way that they do. One of them is already protesting and let's hope it fails to convince the other three to join it."

"Carl, I am walking as fast as I can. Just make way for me to lump myself down before crashing on to you. Remember I told you yesterday not to worry that you will be fine. Now let's hear what Carl is excited about."

"Grandpa, our Princess nearly choked up on her feed. I could not control my laughter last night as she struggled to throw out the stuff from her throat. You should see h…"

"Hold on a minute Carl, did you try to help her, or at least offer her water to drink? It might be helpful to simply stroke the spine region. Common, what did you do to help her? And what did Mr. Smith and Budo do to help her?"

"Help Princess! What are you talking about grandpa? I was afraid of her biting me otherwise my plan was to shove in some more feed down her throat. But I was more amused seeing her eyes bulging and almost popping out of her eye sockets. You should have seen that. Very funny indeed!"

"Carl, I don't think it as being funny. You know, she could choke to death that way."

"Even as she was choking, she was eyeing me in her usual mischievous way, and I am sure if I had come near enough to help her she would have hurt me badly. Grandpa, how long and sharp are your toe nails. Let me see. I can't even attempt to lift this huge leg of yours. But compared to Princess, your toe nails are not bad at all. Her toe nails are like the fishing hooks. Curved and sharp. Once I had a fight with her and that was to be the last time I was at arm's length to her. Do you know what she did? She sat on her hock, held her two front legs in front of her chest. I was scared to death. Shivering, I could feel those ten toe nails and the entire teeth in her mouth prominently displayed in front of me. With those deadly eyes and her hissing sound, I could not stand her for a second. As I turned to walk away from her in fears, she lurched at me and sunk those ten nails on my waist and tore my flesh. If I hadn't acted swiftly she would have buried those sharp teeth into my flesh as well. Worst still she would pounce onto my face and blind me. As quickly as she did it she was up on top of her perch far beyond my reach. Not that I would have fought back, if you think of it. It wasn't funny, grandpa."

"Carl, I now see with you as to why you couldn't think of helping her with the choking incident. But what did Budo and Mr. Smith do to help her? I don't think she is that bad to them? And by the way why did she choke in her feed?

"Grandpa, Budo is in his own world all the time. I don't think that he knew what was happening to Princess. He was more interested in not only snatching what was left in Princess' bowl but also the stuff she was throwing up. That's how much he loved to eat. As for Mr. Smith, he was lying down in his room mumbling what I could not understand and laughing out aloud occasionally not knowing what was happening to Princess. He came home last evening stumbling upon things in the house as usual and that's how the whole drama started. This morning he was in good mood as ever, as though nothing had happened. Hey, there he comes, grandpa. I shall see you again tomorrow with more stories. I really enjoyed myself yesterday, and I am sure Princess learned, her good lessons, yesterday."

"Bye Carl, and see you tomorrow."

I can see he is really happy. Sometimes that will help him deal with what he considered as a thorn in the flesh where Princess is concerned. I think he was very eager to narrate the Princess incidence to me which was why he was early to the park today. Hope to hear more tomorrow. It is hard to keep pace with this younger generation and I am glad to be involved in his interests.

"Hey Carl, you look very handsome in that hair-cut. Who is the groomer who styled you so well?" Hope you enjoyed the trip. I always longed for an opportunity to be pampered and spoiled by a groomer. What do you think?"

"Grandpa let me play with my playmates and then come to you later. It seems they are missing me because for quite some time now, I did not meet them at all because of Princess. Bye and see you soon."

"Bye Carl! Enjoy with your mates. Hope to see you soon"

So, nice of him and what a devotion to his playmates. I think he also would like to show off his new hair styling to his play mates. Oh! What a sweet, gentle breeze coming from the lake. My eyelids appear to be getting heavier and heavier. A little nap will do me a lot of good.

CHAPTER SIX

I COULD NOT BELIEVE that I slept so long on this park bench last evening. Guess I was the only one in the park at a point in time before I woke up. Luckily Carl did not get to see me all alone and of course snoring. He is quite right. Mrs. Jones also observed that I snore too loud these days. I think Carl nailed it to old age and I find it hard to think that age is actually catching up on me. My vision is not as good as I believe it was before Carl ridiculed me for not seeing his Frisbee fly past me the first time he met me. But I was getting convinced that my vision was playing tricks with me. It was hard for me not to be in denial of that fact. May be, he was right about not wanting to get old or acknowledge the fact that age is really catching up with me. The other day he remarked that the sound of my snore was too loud and yet I did not hear it. Maybe he is right to suggest that I should have my hearing checked. The younger generations know a lot better than I do even though I am in denial again of that fact. Carl, I know is very witty by nature, but I am beginning to think that I could benefit more from his unbiased way of thinking. I cannot get him to live in my past but at the same time I cannot afford not to live in his present. There he comes! I really like his hair styling. Hope I don't forget to enquire about Princess and her choking incident.

"Carl, nice to see you today. Why is your freebee no longer flying up to this end of the park? I know that you are in the park with your playmates and was waiting for the freebee to direct you to my spot."

"Grandpa my playmates changed the direction of the freebee by directing it far into the lake.

I really don't like fetching objects from the lake. But Labret loves that game. You know when the younger owners are involved in the throw and fetch game they always come up with odd ideas."

"Who is Labret and why is the lake thing fascinating to him, sonny?"

"Grandpa have you forgotten my name already? I am Carl, remember but feel free with me. Labret is very quiet and friendly. He likes to make friends with all the park users. They like the way he moves around everyone gently, wagging his tail from side to side and never tired of doing so. He is very gentle with all the kids in the park. Nothing excites him to bark and I am sure that he welcomes everyone, good or bad, into his house with or without the permission of his owner. We all feel very peaceful around him."

"So you like Labret. Bring him to grandpa and chat with me. I like those who are nice to you."

"I like Labret when we play throw and fetch on the ground with the older owners, but with the younger ones comes the lake game which I never tried. Labret likes anything that generates joy and happiness. On the ground, he runs fast but not like me."

"Why not faster than you sonny no, Carl? Are you sure you are not…?"

"No, no grandpa, I am not lying to you. Labret is much larger than me and you know very well that being that big limits your ability to run faster. I am sure you are aware of this fact by your own experience. The younger owners keep throwing the freebee farther and farther into the lake and Labret keep fetching it full of joy without complaining. By the time the game is over you could see he is completely exhausted. He then joins our playmates and does the only one thing which I don't like."

"And what might that be sonny no Carl? Don't tell me to throw him out of the park for that reason."

"No grandpa, not that bad. All he does soon after joining us is to shake his massive body thereby splashing water on all of us. He does that many times to dry himself up and get rid of water that entered his ear canal. I don't like getting wet and that in the reason I hate jumping into the lake. More than that, I do not know how to swim. I don't want to drown in the lake."

"Don't be so timid, Carl. We all know how to swim. All you do while in the lake is to keep your head above the water and paddle away with your legs. Try that once and you will agree with what I am telling you."

"Grandpa, have you ever tried to swim in the lake? I think you will sink to the bottom of the lake if you try to swim because you are too…"

"No, not at all, sonny Carl. Don't know why I cannot recall this nice simple name easily. Am I really that old and forgetful now? My being too bulky or whatever you want to call it, will not prevent me from keeping my head above the water and paddle with my powerful legs. Anyway, try and bring Labret to say hi to grandpa, OK?"

"And one more thing, grandpa, about Labret is that he likes to socialise with all the park users and they all want his attention. So, walking up to you will take much longer time far beyond what my patience could handle. But I will try to bring him to you because you are very accommodating and nice to me. I don't know how you are able to tolerate me. Many think, that I am witty, arrogant and try to avoid me. I think they are right but I like to speak my mind and I am always right, am I not, grandpa?"

"Oh yes you are. To be frank, you are the best! Carl. I must admit that since knowing you, I have learnt so many things from you, which I am proud of. By the way, how is Princess coping with the choking incident? What really happened that made her choke in her feed?"

"I told you the story, last time. Oh! No! have you forgotten again grandpa?"

"No you did not because you had to leave with Mr. Smith just as you were about to start the story. But I am happy for you because you were really in a very happy mood on that day, sonny no Carl."

"Never mind, grandpa, I can tell that story any number of times and still feel happy doing so because she deserved to learn lessons in bitter ways sometimes. This is how it happened. Mr. Smith came in last evening in his usual light mood, humming to himself and every now and then stumbling upon things on his pathway. It was time for our dinner. He displayed our bowls on the floor. Normally he places Princess' small bowl and fills it with her feed which happens to be the small bits. Next to hers is my medium bowl and then Budo's much larger bowl and fills them with our feed which is of larger bits compared to Princess' "

"Then what happened, Carl? Why did Princess choke on her feed? That's what I am curious to hear."

"Grandpa, I am coming with the facts, but before that please concentrate so you don't miss the point. Do you actually act more or less impatient as you grow older? Like I was saying before you interrupted me, Mr. Smith came in more confused than ever or should I say size blind. This time around he placed my medium bowl on the floor first and filled it with the feed meant for Princess. In the small and the large bowl, he put the large crumps meant for Budo and I. Grandpa do you now understand where my facts are heading to"?

"Yes I do, Carl but what did you do? Did you try to correct the mistake and eat what was in Princess' bowl?

"Grandpa, I am always not confused and I am not size blind. As soon as Mr. Smith left the dinner room I charged for my medium bowl and its content. Not much but really delicious. Budo settled with his large bowl. You should see the look on Princess' face. She got to taste my feed for the first time."

"That's a very unfortunate mistake, Carl. And how did her feed taste to you? Did you enjoy it?"

"Of course I did. I have always wanted to taste it in the past just for the rich flavour. What Budo and I get is nothing compared to the quality Princess gets. That's why she thinks she is the boss and I don't know why Mr. Smith favours her in everything. Grandpa, is it fair for Mr. Smith to act that way? What is so special about Princess, I do not know."

"Carl did Budo enjoyed his feed? From what I gathered so far, the Princess feed which you mistakenly received was very delicious but what did Princess do?"

"Who cared for what she did. I quickly finished her feed which was on my bowl but not without nodding towards her from time to time to appreciate delicacy of her feed. Grandpa, I am sure she hated me more for that but I enjoyed every moment of the situation."

"Then what happened? Carl, you are fond of delaying on main issue. What did she do?"

"She kept chewing on my feed in her bowl with disgust. At the same time, she maintained a steady gaze on me. I was enjoying myself at her expense. To irritate her more I started tossing her bowl gently while I positioned myself safely right behind Budo. Grandpa, do you know what she did? She lurched at me but unfortunately for her the big Budo was in the way of her attack so she could not reach me. In that process the large feed bits in her mouth shoved down the throat the wrong way I believe. She fell to the ground short of my reach and started coughing violently, drooling from her mouth. In the mean Budo helped himself to the feed left in her now medium bowl and at the same time keenly waiting to see how to feast on her vomit. Having finished the delicious portion on my bowl I maintained a safe distance from Princess behind Budo. She was coughing, painfully as I can observe, to my pleasure. Grandpa Budo can eat anything. He had no clue what was happening to Princess. At least I did and was interested on the outcome."

"Poor Princess, she must have felt horrible and sickened. How did she finally get over, Carl?"

"To my displeasure, Mr. Smith came and… you know grandpa, Budo's feed bowl is many times the size of my bowl and he wallops the feed completely before I even started at mine. Sometimes I always wonder how large yours must be. Many times, Bubo's bowl in the least. Or do you have to feed directly from the feed bin itself."

"Carl it is now your turn to concentrate and finish the story. And my humble question is, how did Princess get over her sickness?"

46

"Grandpa I told you a while ago that Mr. Smith was alerted and carried her away even though he wasn't very firm on his feet. What I like so much about you is your kind and soft hearted nature. Don't worry, Princess is fully recovered but now twice as mischievous. I didn't tell you she was sick, grandpa. She choked in her feed."

"Yes I know. But she was really sick and could have choked to death if Mr. Smith didn't help out."

"OH yes, you are right. Now back to my question on how large your feed bowl is. You know grandpa when Mr. Smith picks after me he does so easily with one hand but for Budo's poop he must leave his cigarette between his lips, bend down on knees and dig it up with both hands. Each time he looks at Budo and says "oh no Budo!" I always observed how he usually shifted his nose in a different direction doing so."

"Yes Carl I know that the next question coming to me will be how heavy my …"

"Yes exactly Grandpa, but how do you know to read my mind. You are really smart and wise. So, who picks after you and how is the poop transported to the waste bin. What a task, grandpa!"

"Let me put it this way for you Carl. My feed bowl is large enough to allow ten like Carl access to feed at the same time comfortably without their heads touching doing so. As for my poop let me leave to your imagination for now. Food for thought. By the way, you look very nice the way you are now. Your groomer did a very good job styling your hairs.

"Don't even talk about it, grandpa. That's a whole lot to talk about. Princess, Budo and I were taken to the… oh, there comes Mr. Smith. I have to leave you now. Bye grandpa, see you tomorrow."

"Bye Carl and nice talking to you. Hope to see you again tomorrow. But don't forget that you just started telling about your hair styling. Not finished yet, remember"

"I will grandpa, bye."

What a day! But I really enjoyed talking to Carl and listening to his story. I look forward to bringing a positive change in him to make him appreciate Princess. As for the vet, it will be an uphill task to convince Carl that the poor vet is actually on his side trying to make him live a long and healthy life. But as long as the vet has to do his work for which he is paid, most of the time he has to inflict a necessary pain on Carl. A necessary pain indeed for which he will never earn Carl's forgiveness. It's getting late I have to get home as quickly as I can and take Mrs. Jones for a short walk. I will never forget how Mr. Jones pushed me around in the baby pram daily, to and from the park. Not a day went by that we didn't visit the park as long as the weather permitted. As for Mrs. Jones, all that I do is to walk by her side wherever she decides to go. Few steps and she is stopped by an acquaintance for formal greetings and brief discussions. She has many such friends in the neighbourhood who also extend their compliments to me as well. Because of her, I earn a lot of admiration and importance. It is a pleasure and I look forward to it every day.

CHAPTER SEVEN

THE PARK IS FULL OF many unfamiliar faces today and I wonder what is going on. Once in a while fun fairs are staged here that attract park users from far and wide taking part in various events. A good number of us are on leash. From time to time I can hear barking and high pitched voices which I believe are meant to intervene when things go wrong. This brings back a lot of bad memories of the days some of us are denied the honour of basic freedom to move around in this park unleashed. And to think that such is the situation in many other parks is very pathetic and has to change. And for that change to occur we have to change our attitude completely and learn the art of peaceful co-existence. We must look upon violence as evil, learn to appreciate one another before we can earn the trust and respect from the humans. Carl and his friend Labret, I am afraid, might attempt to befriend some of these strange ones and fall into harm's way. They are not used to violence in this park. I wish I had the opportunity to advise Carl to stay safe in the park, today in particular. Oh, there he comes. He looks worried. It does not look like all is fine with him. He appears to be frequently looking back to make sure that his tail is still in place and not under threat from some of us in the park today.

"Eh grandpa, what's going on in the park today? Why are so many of us on leash in the park today? Leash festival or what? I was expecting to see you on leash today as well. Mr. Smith was scared when he learnt that I was coming up here to meet you. Scared of my safety for the first time in this park."

"Carl I was equally worried about your safety as well. I know that you are not used to this kind of events happening in this park. It is called park fun fair in which park users come here with their families to play around. As far as I know this is the third time I observed it in this park. The last one happened a long time ago. I remember lying safely inside the baby pram under the watchful eyes on Mr. Jones. He kept me safe and I wish I had the chance of protecting you as well today. Glad you are safe and just be vigilant. Some of us are not friendly to one another as you can see in the park today."

"I was playing fetch with my mates, grandpa and all of a sudden the strange ones in the park got very excited, started barking, running angrily towards us only to be restrained by their owners who held them tight on the leash. We were forced to abandon our fetch game for the sake of peace.

That's not fair, grandpa. Why should they be angry with us for playing our game and not inviting them?"

"Carl I understand how you feel but today is a special day for the humans and may not happen again here in a very long, long time."

"But that not fair grandpa. My playmates and I got disbanded. I was minding my own business, on my way to see you, when one of us, got upset and charged towards me. He was much smaller than I am. As he approached I stopped to see what he was up to. He started circling around me and sniffing my rear end. I got equally upset with him and wanted to decapitate him. The cold growl from the depth of my stomach was obvious to his owner that I am capable inflicting severe damage to him if not restrained. The owner dragged him back before that happened. Even after that I could still hear him barking. Today is really wasted for me and my playmates, grandpa."!!!!!!!!!!!!!

"Don't you worry, it will not happen again in a long, long time. Now let's hear about your visit to your groomer. Such a nice job was done on you, Carl. I am sure you enjoyed the entire process."

"Grandpa is it true that as we get older the hairs on our body fall off gradually and steadily until we become totally bald all over our body?" that means that by the time I become very old like you are now I will lose all my hairs. When that happens, Mr. Jones will not take me to her again."

"Why Carl? What happened to you. I was happy for you thinking that you enjoyed being pampered at the salon."

"Don't tell me, grandpa that you have forgotten your own experiences with the groomer when you were younger and your huge body covered with hairs. I can't wait to lose the hairs on my body if that means not going to her for anything again."

"It appears to me that all didn't go well with you at the salon. But you look very nice and smell fresh, Carl. What happened to you there.?"

"Grandpa, Mr. Smith will never allow us to decide for ourselves when it comes to our hairs. Occasionally, while serving us dinner, he will say 'Princess, Carl, Budo, I think your hairs need some attention. They are flying all over the place. Princess you keep licking your body all the time swallowing hairs in the process and throwing up hair balls in your vomit. Carl and Budo I can see that you are feeling uncomfortable and always scratching your body. This happens when large amount of dead old hairs need to be replaced by new hair growth. I think it's time to visit your groomer to clean you up and make you look and smell fresh. I know the visits to the groomer, to be specific not always pleasant but at the end you will all feel much better. Carl, your annual show competition is taking place soon. We must look nice and presentable to participate and enjoy the event, don't we?' At that I know what…"

"Hold on Carl, what annual show is Mr. Smith talking about and what competition are you taking part in?"

"Ok, grandpa let me believe that I have never mentioned to you that I take part in the run and fetch event but I am quite sure that you are aware of our show that is conducted in different places. I train hard for the event that's why I practice with my play mates in this park daily. See how I have wasted today's practice because of these new visitors to the park today. Grandpa do you think that I will not be able to train in the park tomorrow because of these visitors?"

"Don't worry Carl, they will not be here tomorrow. You will have the park to yourselves tomorrow and I am definite about it. Of course, I know about our shows conducted in many different places but it has never taken place near or close enough for me to observe or take part in any of the events. It is good to know that you are actively involved and taking part in the competitions."

"Grandpa I don't simply take part in the event but I am always a winner. Once I come out for my event the humans will be screaming, 'Carl! Carl!! Carl!!!...' I am very popular and always a winner. It is not that the competitions are easy. They are really tough and you have to compete with the best at every event. Do you think you will be able to participate in any competitive events at our show? You know Budo does not take part in any event because he is too big to run as fast as required. But if there is an eating competition you will win. There is no doubt about that but you will face a stiff challenge from Budo."

"Carl let say that I may not be able to compete with you in the run and fetch event, but do you know in what event I can out smart you?"

"Grandpa don't even think of it. What event, outside the eating competition, which is yet to be included in the competition will you be able to compete with me? Let's consider other events like rope skipping, dancing, obedience test."

"Carl, are those the only events that happen at the competition?"

"No grandpa, there are pole dodging, swim and fetch, the obstacle events where you have to run and hop over obstacle bars. That sort of thing. There are many more which you may not be able to compete in. At one time Budo showed some interest to take part in an event and become a winner like me. He entered for the pole dodging event. At the starting line Mr. Smith, decided to motivate him to stay focused and do the race. He does not have to run like I do. All he needed to do was walk his way, fast enough of course in a zigzag way through wooden posts mounted at equal distance at a straight line, without knocking the posts down. At the start of his turn to the event Mr. Smith offered him a piece of cookie. While he chewed on the cookie, he entered the ring and by the time he got to the middle of the ring he stopped and wanted more cookies. He wouldn't move a step unless his mouth is stuffed with more cookie. Nothing would make him take another step until he got the treat. The humans kept yelling and bowing at him but he wouldn't care. Instead he slumped right in front of Mr. Smith staring at the cookies in his hand. Finally, he left the area only after he got his demand without completing the event. That happened to be his first and last stake at any event. It is hard grandpa, to compete in an event.

Just like Budo, I don't think you can handle the pressure in competing."

"Carl, that's very funny for Budo to behave that way but, may be, he was really hungry before and during the event. But can you think of any event that grandpa can, not only compete in but will emerge as the winner instead of Carl?"

"I don't think so. Not in any of the events happening at the show unless I voluntarily decided to grant you the winning opportunity as a big favour grandpa."

"OK Carl, picture that you are at the lead with about dozen Carls lined behind you and you are required to pull at one end of a strong rope while grandpa was to pull at the other end of the rope. Between your team and grandpa, a line is drawn on the ground at the middle separating our team and grandpa. At the stroke of the bell the team that drags the other across the line wins the competition."

"Grandpa there is no…"

"Yes Carl there is an event in our called 'Tug-Of-War' do you remember? Grandpa will, surely drag all of you rolling on the ground across the line in no time and emerge the winner very easily. Do you think that I am capable of winning in that event?"

"Ok, grandpa, yes I just remembered that I have not told you what happened at the grooming salon. This is what happened. As usual Mr. Smith took the three of us to the groomer totally against our will. The groomer hates me and I know it very well. But she adores Princess and likes Budo."

"Hold on Carl, first grandpa will win in the event and we both agreed on that. Why is it that she does not like you but did such a nice job on your hair? May be, you don't like her instead."

"There is nothing to like about going to her, grandpa. Not when I think of the tugging and pulling on my hair which is very painful. She wouldn't let me decide how to position myself on the table. At one time, she stretches my leg forward and at another drags it backwards while combing and brushing hairs in sequence. She pulled the hairs in my ears, cuts my toe nails short making it difficult to scratch myself. Instead I have to drag myself to objects to ease off itches. She bathes in in warm water which I like very much if the soap does not get into my eyes or ears. Finally the blow-drying thing which is not only noisy but frightening. She will keep on doing the blow drying non-stop completely ignoring my scream. At one time, I was screaming so loud that even Princess felt pity for me and started crying." Then talk about the hairy combing and clipping. It is horrible experience, grandpa, horrible to say the least. The process lasts far too long for my liking."

"But she does the same to Princess and Budo as well, so Carl why is yours different? I think you have to be a little more cooperative with her while she does the job. Remember Mr. Smith pays her for the job."

"Yes, I know grandpa but with Princess, she keeps singing to her and Princess likes that. But once in a while Princess gets angry at her and even tries to scratch or bite her. At that she lets Princess take a break and then continue. But for me she yields at me but will never let me take a break. Sometimes she even threatens me. That makes me more, angry."

"What happens when she grooms Budo?"

"Grandpa, I told you that Budo will do anything for food. When he feels upset she shove some cookies down his throat. With that he is ok. As long as he keeps chewing on food he is fine. Remember grandpa, Budo has very short hairs on his body and does not experience the tugging, pulling and prolonged blow-drying of the hairs like I do. But where Budo is concerned, do not touch his legs to clip his nails short. His resistance is such that you might as well slit his throat right through but never try to cut his nails. That will be his resistance level. This is the only time you cannot calm Budo down with food. Let go his feet and the nail clipper and he would eat up anything offered to him including the bowl when he is that hunger. And he is always hungry. Of course, he is not as bald, as you are now but I am sure that he will look just as bald when he got old. Still a very long time for him to get to that stage. Very, very long time indeed. But for me, I could not be calmed down with food. All I want is to be left alone. She does not realise how painful it is to, detangle my hair and to be restrained on that table for a very long time. I rather prefer to be out here in the park in the company of my playmates. That's why she does not like me, I think."Her bathing me is the only thing I enjoy because the water is just warm enough to sooth my skin."

'In that case Carl, just be satisfied with the bathing session and simply forget the brushing and combing process. I would do anything to enjoy a nice, soapy warm water bath. I wouldn't complain at all for that."

"Grandpa, I am sure you will like the bath but what about the hair treatment that follows? After the bath, she towelled me dry but that didn't end there. Do you know what she did next?"

"What next Carl?"

"Carl, did I hear you say that Princess cried seeing you in agony? I find it hard to believe you just said that. That means she has a very soft spot for you in her heart. Like Mr. Smith and I said you have to give Princess a chance to show her good side which I think you will definitely fall for."

"Grandpa, do you mean what you just said or are you simply pulling my legs? I am beginning to think in that direction. But wait a second, am I just talking in my dreams or am I real? You know grandpa, you might be right. After that choking incident she will always leave some left-over feed in her bowl but will never allow Budo to eat it. At the same time, she kept a gaze at me. I do not know what her intentions are but I am smarter than she is and always kept my distance from her and her feed bowl."

"Carl, you still don't get it. Princess knew that you relished eating her feed on the day she choked on yours. She now wants you to continue enjoying the treat from her bowl. All she wants you to do is to eat it. As such she is extending a warm friendship to you. So, Carl go for it and believe me you will never regret doing so."

"Grandpa, you are joking with me now. I think the left-over feed in her bowl is more like a bait and I am not falling for it. I like her feed but I cannot risk those sharp toe nails of hers embedded under my skin, not to mention those razor-sharp teeth of hers. I am sure I am too smart for her to trick me. Just forget that idea, grandpa."

"Please yourself Carl, but I am sure that you will sometime benefit from my wisdom. Princess wants to extend her friendship to you. Take it or leave it. And so, continue with your story. What happened at the groomer?"

"Where did I stop grandpa? Oh, yes, that blow dryer almost deafened me. Then came another round of brushing and combing. That's when I lost it and couldn't take it any longer."

"What did you do then, Carl?"

"Grandpa, I am powerless before that groomer and Mr. Smith will always take us to that salon. She will talk nicely to him and will be full of praises about us. But as soon as he goes away everything changes. She terrifies me. The first time we there she started acting funny with me and I showed her what Carl is capable of doing."

"I can only imagine what you are capable of, Carl, but how did you get away with it?"

"When you were small and young like me, grandpa did you always allow yourself to be bullied without fighting back? I mean, have you ever bitten someone when they get at your wrong side and try to mess around you? Oh! I always forget that you have no hairs to be messed up with, but those big toe nails of yours needed trimming from time to time?"

'Carl when I was your age Mr. Jones trained me not to bite humans and I never did. It is very cruel to do so."

"I know and you are right grandpa. But she failed to take my warnings seriously. For example, I try to make eye contact with her to warn her but she ignores it. I have no choice but to react and when I do, I make sure I do a good job of it."

"Do you mean to tell me that you bit the groomer the very first time you went to her, Carl? Don't you realise that she was only doing her job which Mr. Smith instructed her to do? That was not fair to attack her"

"Grandpa, you may not like what I do to avoid being on that table longer than necessary. May be necessary to develop a trick, technique, system or whatever will work. I make biting my last resort. How about that? But grandpa, she was smarter than I was. She muzzled me up when I eye-balled and growled at her, displaying my tightly clenched teeth to her. She knew what I could have done if my mouth was let loose as it should be. These humans are really smarter than we are, don't you think so? But with Budo she could not succeed in muzzling him to trim his nails without risking, you know what grandpa. I know you will be wondering, if muzzling worked with Carl why not with Budo to get his toe nails clipped? But wait until you see Budo. You know grandpa the groomer can easily and successfully muzzle you up with her eyes completely closed. That is not the case with Bodu. Wait until you see him and his facial structure. Only then you will understand."

"But I still maintain we have to listen to the humans and try to learn from them. They do everything for us. All that they want in return is the obedience that will enable us fit into their world. I think it will be rude to reward them by inflicting injuries on them. Don't you see with me, Carl?"

"In a way, yes you are right grandpa but when they keep hurting us like the groomer always does to me, the only way to defend myself is to …"

"Is to do what? Bite her? That was wrong Carl. Our mouth is there only to send food down to the stomach in order to stay alive and healthy. Otherwise it is there to bark to ward off intruders and alert the humans of unpleasant situation. Of course, when we are hot inside panting with our mouth wide open helps us stay cooler inside. Never to bite them for any reason, Carl. That is what Mr. Jones taught me. I would like you to learn that from me hereafter."

"Do you know what, grandpa? It is no longer possible for me anymore to use my mouth in any way because as soon as Mr. Smith drops us off at the salon, my mouth is tied up as she places me on her grooming table or whatever she thinks she is doing with it. All I do is to resist any process I do not approve of. The other day one of us was on her table, smaller than me, with long hair but more patient than I am. She kept on pulling and tugging on his hair while we watched waiting for our turn. When he could no longer bear the pain he started crying in a very melodious tone. I felt very sorry for him and so did the rest of us trapped in her cage."

"How did you and the rest of you react, Carl to help him out"?

"Grandpa, I could not bear it much longer as I felt tears welling in my eyes. I joined his chorus so melodiously that one after another the rest of us joined in. She could not help yelling 'stop that all of you, stop now, stop I say' but no one listened and our song vibrated in the salon until she stopped tormenting him. Out of fears he stopped crying and one after the other the rest of us withdrew but still I was not satisfied. I continued while the others stared at me in astonishment but I was not bothered until I came up with an idea to halt her process."

"Do you know what Carl? You all in that salon could for a musical group, I am sure that the humans would like to be entertained by a musical group lead by no other Carl."

"Grandpa that is not funny. We were all aware that our turn on the table cannot be avoided. It actual was a kind of peaceful protest but she cared less."

"I was only teasing you Carl, but you have to remember that she was doing what your owners, if I may use that term, desired. She is also being paid to groom you all to look good and smell fresh. It hurts no doubt but the humans like us better that way. What type of process are you referring to, Carl which you don't approve of?"

"If you have not forgotten already, I mean such processes like plucking hairs off from my ear canal, lifting up my legs in order to reach and shave my groin areas, not to mention tugging and pulling on my hairs, clipping my toe nails. Grandpa these are not only very painful but unnecessary to me. I would prefer to be left alone. Not for her to lift my legs when she wants to and not when I want to. I am comfortable with the hairs growing inside my ear canal. The hairs in my ear canal do not affect my hearing. They actually help to prevent tiny insects entering my ear. Why would she decide to pull them off and hurt me in the process? I like it when she baths me because until she does so, I get very itchy and perceive the bad odour in me which is very uncomfortable. But after the bathing I wish she could let me dry myself up instead of the using that deafening blow dryer on me."

"But remember Carl, she cannot cut your hairs and make you look as nice as you are now without first bathing and drying your hairs. And it takes a long time to do so, I agree. You know, when your hair is dirty, it will smell awful and irritate your skin. You will end up with rashes on your body. Would you like that to happen to you?"

"Grandpa, I know all that and I now discovered another trick that works but will not hurt the groomer at the same time. Whenever, I get the slightest hint from Mr. Smith we will be going to visit the groomer, do you know what I do?"

"No Carl, what order tricks are you up to?"

"Grandpa, I save up the poop inside me, and that morning Mr. Smith will not have to pick after me. He will ask 'Carl, what's wrong with you today, no poops? I would reply I'm ok. Budo's will do for today."

"And how does that help you when you get to the … oh! no Carl, don't make me think that you are up to what I am imagining now."

"You know grandpa, you are full of wisdom that comes with old age because I am sure that when you were my age you were not smart enough to plan line of action, the way I do. I am sure you would expect me to plug my anus because I am visiting the groomer. This technique works for me and this is how. While on her table she ties my mouth. This time I readily thrust it forward for her to reach and muzzle it up. No struggles. I allow her to do as she pleases without resisting or complaining, but as soon as she reaches for my leg to lift it up I could feel the gas tunnelling down my rectum reaching for an exit. As soon as I let the gas exit the tunnel she screams her lungs out shouting 'oh No! Carl, what on earth did Mr. Smith feed you today?' Believe me I do not enjoy the smell at all myself. But she deserves every ounce of it."

"Oh but that clears off fast and what happens after, Carl?"

"Grandpa I am not so stupid to let the tunnel open all at a time. Remember, the control valve of my tunnel is directly under my control and I let go when and as needed. But I make sure that I do not run out of gas until I am let down the table. I also make sure that I let off the last traces of the gas as soon as Mr. Smiths, enters the salon to take us home. He also should partake in the gas festival for bringing us here. Trust me, I don't think he enjoys the air in the room either.

But somehow he is entertained in the gas festival, as I prefer to call it, briefly, but unfortunately that is not strong enough to discourage him from bringing us here."

"Smart idea Carl, but I could not imagine how you came up with this idea to begin with. You are really a genius sonny, but how did you achieve your goal finally?"

"Grandpa, each time I let go, you could hear her screaming 'no Carl, stop Carl, bad boy Carl, it's hard to continue, enough is enough now get down and get lost, bad boy!' As soon as I am down from the table, I move to the farthest hideout and observe situations as they develop. But on the whole I am sure that it cuts my time on the grooming table to a reasonable extent which I very much appreciate. Above all I no longer try to harm or threaten the groomer in the process and she stopped muzzling me. That in itself is a mutual win situation for she and me isn't it grandpa?"

"You are really very smart to think your way out of what seems a difficult situation even though it is somehow cruel. But how did Princess and Budo feel about the salon?"

"I know that I am very smart, grandpa. All my playmates refer to me as the smartest and they are right. I am glad you confirmed it too. Before I came up with how best to deal with the groomer, I tried many tricks like showing off my tightly clenched but muzzled teeth with the most unfriendly stare, the blood curdling growl from the depth of my gut. None of those tricks paid off. Then I tried to act in the most uncooperative manner towards her every attempt to restrain me. For instance, whenever she tried to raise my foot, I pull it down. When she wants me to stand freely on my four legs, I make it a point to lay on my belly. Sometime when I stick my very own tongue out to pant normally she tries to push it back to avoid nicking it. That's when I forcibly stick out the entire length of my tongue. Somehow she outwitted my tricks. Finally, I ran out of tricks but did not give up."

"Then what happened, Carl?"

"Grandpa, maybe I have asked you this question before but I am very curious for an answer to it now."

"Yes Carl, what is it you that are curious to know from me?"

"When and how did you lose all the hairs on your body and become bald?"

"Carl maybe I have explained this to you before. If not, the answer to your question is that I was born hairless, lived up to date hairless and will definitely die hairless. You are too young to understand what I am telling you now, but what is the connection between the hairs on my body and your regular trip to the salon?"

"This is the reason why I always consider myself too smart and more intelligent than all of us. One day Mr. Smith took us to the salon for the usual hair styling. On the table was a huge one like you. The difference is that his ears are even shorter than mine and in nowhere close to those massive leaves sticking out of your head, grandpa. They are even much smaller than mine which I think is quite unusual. I would do anything for a fair exchange with you for those ears. If I have those ears I would sleep more soundly. I would flap them over my eyes to screen off the lights while I sleep. Or fan them across my nose to dispel foul smell."

"And remember with my type you can as well fan the flies off your face when needed. Carl, what are you arriving at?"

"Grandpa picture this and try to concentrate while doing so.

At the salon, this huge one was on the table and she was simply taking life out of him. I am referring to the groomer or whatever you choose to call her. From the look of things, he was barely tolerating her and the pain he was going through especially with the tugging and pulling of his hairs. To my greatest surprise he was not revolting in any way. But instead, for example, at a mere touch of his leg, he simply lifts it up without her asking so that she could probe his groins at will. Keeps it up in the air as long as she wants, in return all she does is to keep on praising him saying 'good boy, yes I know it is painful boy, you are almost done boy, Daddy will be happy with you and give you some treats when we are done. Good boy."

"What finally happened with Bouv Carl?"

"Grandpa, how do you know his name is Bouv without me telling you? All the while I was saying "boy" and not "Bouv" but this time your imagination work perfect and accurate."

"I am equally smart like you if not smarter and I know there are not many huge ones like me around, Carl. That name is very familiar to me. Sometime ago, a huge one like me but hairy came to this park and the owner was so fond of him that she was calling the name Bouv all the time. I saw both of then, once but his appearance is hard for me to forget especially with his long, bushy hairs all over his body including his face. At that time, I was more concerned about how he is able to move around freely with those long hairs across his face. So, Carl what is the connection?"

"No grandpa. No one is smarter than I am. This is what happened. After the brushing on the table which took a long time, she gave Bouv a bath and brought him back to the table for drying. The blow dryer she was using was very noisy and I am sure Bouv wasn't pleased with the sound as she aims the dryer nuzzle on his legs, neck, body, head, back etc. I was keenly observing Bouv's reaction from the inside of my cage wondering why Bouv is not using his personality to intimidate her. I would have done so if it was me but as she moved towards his bum area things changed. Bouv became more uncomfortable stance with the drying progression towards his rear end. Finally, he took the usual stance to ease himself but not the normal lifting of the rear leg. Instead he lowered his back and moved his hind quarters sideways a couple of times, our usual way of doing things and before you know it, he dumped a load on the table to my surprise."

"What, Carl? Bouv did it on the grooming table as he was being dried! What was her reaction?"

"All she kept shouting was 'No Bouv no. But it was already too late to interrupt Bouv's action. I don't think I would dump such heavy load for many days combined. Anyway, she cleared the mess and resumed the blow drying. But unfortunately, it happened a second and third time whenever she progressed towards his bum area. Out of frustration of having to clear and clean up the mess on her table she gave up, brought Bouv down from the table and dragged him into the cage. That done, she came after us. So, what I learned from Bouv's action is helping me now. I realised that the quickest way to be released from the table was to create a very unpleasant situation in the salon. Grandpa I know that you would think it rude on my part but no harm was done to anyone. I don't have to dump a mess on her table to discourage her but instead I can shorten my stay on the table by letting go the access to my tunnel. To my greatest surprised my strategy worked best and I am happy dealing with her that way. What do you think grandpa?"

"Oh that's how you learned your trick, Carl. Very smart indeed, but what about Budo?

"Budo at first did not…hold on a minute grandpa. At the moment, only the two of us are here, isn't it? I am sure that my tunnel control is active and nothing has escaped from it yet. That means…"

"I am not sure what that means but my tunnel is usually opened once in a day and only when I am being picked after.

And if only the two of us are here then something is wrong somewhere. What do you think Carl?"

"Something is wrong somewhere and you are right. Grandpa I wanted you to experience for yourself a similar situation as it happens in the salon. But let me ask if your nose is blocked. Usually it is the case with…"

"You may be tempted to think that everything happens or does not happen because of old age. But, Carl let me ask you this. If you have to run non-stop from here to your competition place, I am sure it will take you many days to get there."

"Grandpa, you have started day-dreaming again. We are talking about the grooming salon and not the competition place. We do not run from home to the place. Mr. Smith usually takes us in his car otherwise by the time we ran to the place we would not be able to compete in any event. Yes, it is far and takes him a little less than half a day to drive us to the place."

"Good to know that, but Carl, did Mr. Smith pick after you today?"

"Yes he did as usual. In fact, he picked more than the usual amount from us today after the big treat yesterday for being nice to Princess."

"Carl you were nice to Princess! That's very interesting and I am sure you will eventually accept her as a friend. Did you agree with me, when I told you she is nice?"

70

"She gradually and steadily became nice and friendly to Budo and I so we allowed her to play with us. Mr. Smith observed us playing together and happily gave us a generous treat yesterday, resulting in greater than normal poop size from both of us, which he unhappily picked. Wait a minute I think I know where you are heading to grandpa!"

"Let me put it this way Carl, I have never been to your competition place but when you get there next I shall pick your scent from here and trace you to that place without any assistance. My greatest strength is in my sense of smell. And so back to my question for which you pointed out that Mr. Smith picked after you today. It appears to me that your weapon was lunched here as usual but it failed to hit the desired target because it was…?

"Oh grandpa, I get your point and I really think that you are not only very smart but very intelligent, full of wisdom and patience. Your nose may not be blocked yet, but you need to have many different functions checked on regular basis especially at your age. Yes, I let off steam from my tunnel but it wasn't as strong as it was meant to be in the salon. The reason being that I did not omit today's poop. Even though I do not want to grow old, I want to be smarter, more intelligent and work on my patience. I think I am wise enough now. Do you agree with me grandpa?"

"Carl you are very smart too. I learn a lot of things by my association with you. You have to grow old sometime, whether you like it or not. And with growing old comes greater tolerance, patience and wisdom. Once again, back to my question. How did Budo and Princess feel at the salon. And by the way I can pick up Mr. Smith's scent as he is approaching us to take you home."

"Grandpa, you have started imagining things again. If Mr. Smith is on his way to pick me up I should be able to see him from afar before you do, because my sight is many times more powerful than yours. I am much younger. Not only that, we still have a long way to go before heading home. So, I am not referring to imagination as a form of wisdom."

"Yes Carl, but I can assure you that over the course of my life time, I have solved so many cases with humans involving tracking down criminals from very far off distances to the amazement of the humans. It is not a matter of imagination as you term it to be. All I needed was to get to the site of the crime, pick up the scent, trail the suspect and successfully lead the human investigators to the suspect's hide out. The ability to do this has nothing to do with smartness, intelligence or wisdom. I inherited it from my original parents who also inherited it from theirs and so on."

"What do you do when you track down the suspect? When you pin the suspect down, grandpa how much injury do you inflict on him before the humans arrive to rescue their loved ones from your massive grip?"

"That's very funny for you to visualise me trying to bite my catch. Unfortunately, Carl, I do the opposite. I treat them as gently as possible and I even lick up the wound or dirt on them. I make sure they remain as safe and comfortable as they would love to before the humans take over. I am never hostile to anyone ever."

"Let me believe you are not pulling my legs grandpa but I still cannot see Mr. Smith. It is too early for us to head home."

"He will be here in no time because his scent is getting stronger and stronger indicating that he is getting closer and closer to us."

"Ok, grandpa let's talk about something else. Yes, Budo and Princess do not feel the same way as I do at the salon because…"

"Hold on to that story till tomorrow because Mr. Smith is right behind you. Turn and have a look Carl."

"You are amazing grandpa. I believe your claims about picking up scent from a distance. I would like to train to pick up scent as well just like you and just like how your parents trained you. Good bye grandpa."

"Goodbye Carl."

That is going to be a difficult one, to convince Carl that certain things cannot be acquired through training. But at the same I like his curiosity and ambition to be good in everything. One great achievement is getting along well with Princess. What I still cannot understand is how he came up with the idea of tackling the groomer. I only hope that he doesn't get unintentionally hurt by the groomer attempting to speed up the grooming process. All, said done Carl is a very interesting character. Now that he has felt the park I need to take a nap before heading home to take Mrs. Jones for the usual evening walk.

CHAPTER EIGHT

IT APPEARS TO ME that there are many new park users this time. From this bench, I get to see all the park users both familiar and new users as they enter the park. Oh, no, that one coming in to the park with mouth tightly muzzled reminds me of Bullie in those days. He used to be on his own all the time, by the side of the owner with mouth tied up. I used to wonder why he was the only one held by the leash all the time. To me he is always minding his own business until one fine day, the ever aggressive and inquisitive Pommi decide to take him to task. I will never forget that day as Pommi kept tormenting, teasing, barking and advancing menacingly towards Bullie until he could take it no more. Bullie leaped up and pinned Pommi to the ground and wouldn't let go despite being tugged and pulled back by the owner. Finally, Pommi escaped the attack bleeding all over after Bullie was successfully pulled away by the owner. Pommi would have been mauled to death if Bullie's mouth wasn't tied up. The incident took the park users like a storm and since then neither Bullie nor Pommi showed up in the park. I must not fail to warn Carl about the new park user. I believe that is not Bullie. But with the mouth tied and leashed at the same time a clear message is out there that he should not be messed around with.

"Carl, come quickly I have something to tell you. Did you see a new park user in here now with mouth tied and leashed by the owner at the same time? Be careful around him. I was just rehearsing within myself an incident that happened here in the park a long time ago. His name was Bullie. He looked just like that new fellow coming into the park leashed, mouth tied, peaceful though but plays with no one. Unfortunately, a much smaller Pommie decided to tease and torment Bullie…"

"Grandpa are you talking about Pitt who came in leashed and mouth tied?"

"Carl, I am referring to the muscular, heavily built …?"

"Yes grandpa. His name is Pitt. He is one of my best playmates. I just got tired playing with him and decided to come and say hi to you. Please don't say anything bad about Pitt. He is very gentle, friendly and I am sure he will never harm anyone. His owner treats him like his own child."

"You may be right Carl, but why is he leashed and muzzled to come to the park?"

"Grandpa, I understand that the humans especially the little ones in his neighbourhood are very hostile and teasing him all the time. Because of that, the owner restrains him around the neighbourhood but as soon as he enters the park he is let loose just like all of my playmates. I know him long before I met you, grandpa."

"But Carl I am seeing him for the first time today. I am only worried for your safety. I am not worried about myself because I can handle any situation."

"He is the first to enter and the last to leave the park because his owner is the in-charge person of this park. So, don't worry about him grandpa. He is well trained and of the best behaviour. I was just telling him that I am going to learn how to pick up scent from a distance from you"

"Yes Carl, but…"

"Grandpa Pitt is equally thrilled about that talent and I wouldn't be surprised if he shows an interest to learn the skill as well. Don't worry he is very friendly, peaceful, and safe to be around with. I am sure you will like him."

"I am happy for you Carl, but what I am trying to explain to about the scent thing is that it is not…"

"Not what grandpa? I confirmed you are capable of picking up scent from a far after you did that with Mr. Smith. I was surprised and impressed at the same time. I am quite sure you mastered that art very well and can teach it as well."

"Thank you Carl for acknowledging ability to pick up scent. We all have that ability and that's one of the many gifts that far exceeds the humans."

"Grandpa do you mean to tell me that the humans cannot pick up scent more than you do? I think the humans are more gifted in everything than we are."

"Carl, like I told you before, when it comes to picking up scent from a distance we are far superior than they are. That's why I helped them in the past to solve many cases requiring picking up scent from far away distances when suspects fled away from crime scenes."

"But I do not have that talent and would like you to teach me all I need to know about it, grandpa. Please do not waste time any longer. We could start right now and I can assure you that being a fast learner I will pick up the talent faster than when you first learned it. My playmates will be surprised when I show them my talent."

"Carl I will willingly and happily teach you whatever I know, but when it comes to picking up smell from a far, that ability is inherited from our parents. The more they have the more they pass onto their off springs at birth. My parents had too much and they passed more to me. Yours have less and they passed less on to you. You cannot be taught how to pick up scent. For instance, my long flappy ears and huge hairless body are some of the things I inherited from them in addition to the scent issue. But I can assure you one thing. Your sense of smell is by far superior to that of the humans. Ok now let's talk about Princess and Budo. I think they enjoyed at the salon. What do you say, Carl?"

"Both of them have no problem at the groomer neither did they enjoy the entire process. There is nothing to enjoy in that salon with the exception of the stress received. Grandpa, I know what your next question will be, and that is, 'why is your own case different?' and the answer is simple. I don't like being forced to do something I found unnecessary like cutting my toe nails which I need to scratch my body, tugging on my hairs as well as the deafening noise from the salon equipment, not to mention the noisy barking from the other ones equally stressed out by her. The last time that we were there, one of us was crying endlessly without any reason until she called the owner to take him home away from the salon. Grandpa you need to go there in order to understand what our experiences are while in the salon."

"But my question remains, how do Princess and Budo handle the salon situation differently from you? May be, you need to learn to adapt in situations like that."

"I think I have learned to adapt in my own way. Grandpa I would like you to look at it this way. She is scared of Princess because of the deadly things Princess is capable of doing with her razor-sharp nails claws and teeth. She lets her have her way most of the time. With Budo, she shoves nice cookies into his mouth whenever necessary to calm him down and will never attempt to clip his toe nails. You can make Budo do anything as long as there is something in front of him to eat. Where I am concerned, none of these tactics will work. And that's why I came up with my tunnel control system. In that case, I am neither barking like the others, aggressive like Princess nor greedy like Budo. Just a peaceful inexpensive demonstration that harms no one but guaranteed positive outcome and early release. These days it's fun for me to visit the salon and observe her reaction when I release my arsenal. I look forward to that fun time in the salon. She really deserves my gas chamber which is guaranteed not to harm her. Just a liberal dose of what I don't need any longer inside me."

"How does she react to all these happening in the salon. She must be mad and confused not knowing how to control all of you. Am I right, Carl?"

"You are right, grandpa. She is always stressed out not knowing how to handle situations. Sometimes there are more than ten of us in the salon, each behaving differently. The barking is always there and endless. But all the same she never loses her patience with us. All she does is keep yelling 'not again Carl; stop that Max; no biting Princess; common Budo, behave yourself; good girl Steff. But unfortunately, we listen and agree with her but continues to behave the same way and even worse. Grandpa if I was in her situation I would be tempted to smack us when situation gets out of control. But she never raised her hand to beat any of us. Instead when our owners arrive to take us home she will be praising all of us."

"Like what Carl?"

"Things like 'Max was such a good boy; Princess is really an adorable girl. She did not threaten anyone; Budo is always as sweet as ever; Carl was well behaved as usual'. She always presented very positive remarks about us. Our owners will take us home with mind-blowing flattery from her not realising what little monsters we had been. As for Mr. Smith, he is easily flattered and would like to go on talking. Little does he realise how stressed out we are. I would hop up to his knees and head toward the exit door and back to him just to let him know we are tired of this place and should be heading home. Unfortunately, he will not like to leave. Finally, I had to release the last gas flow and believe me, grandpa that last streak smells the worst of them all. Only then she will end the conversation just to get rid of me."

"I think she is nice and wonder what makes you think she is not, Carl."

"She is nice but the environment is very stressful, couple with all the things she has to do to make us look better and beautiful to our owners. She is really nice. Hey grandpa! Did I just hear some rumbling somewhere around us? A while ago I heard a very faint sound but this time it is louder. I think your stomach is making that sound. Don't tell me you are about to…"

"No Carl I am not going to fart or whatever you are thinking of. It's just normal for my stomach to rumble at times but it goes away."

"Grandpa Mr. Smith is here to pick me up. When we meet here again I shall let you know how everything went during the show."

"That's ok Carl. I will be missing you throughout the duration of the show, but I am sure you will come first in your event. I will be waiting anxiously to hear about it. Good luck Carl."

"Bye grandpa"

He really trained hard for the coming event and I strongly feel he will win. It will be a long while before I meet him here again. Oh! My stomach is still rumbling again. Mrs. Jones is always looking up to better feed for me. She thinks that there is always a better feed for me and wants me to have the best of the feeds out there. With every new feed introduced my stomach reacts but settles down afterwards. But I must admit that the new feed always tastes better than the previous one. Getting dark already. I better get home as fast as I can.

CHAPTER NINE

IT'S BEEN A LONG time since spoke to Carl and I am beginning to miss him. He did not tell me that the competition takes a long time. It is hard to believe that I have never heard of our show until I met him. Ah! Better not to give him that clue otherwise he would tease me to no end. All said and done I must admit that I have learnt a lot from Carl. I am sure he would have a lot of stories to relay to me when he returns. I can't wait to hear all about the competition. Above all I wish he wins after all the training he went through in preparation for the event. Hey! There goes the busy body Jackie. Why is she always chasing these poor squirrels around in the park? I am sure that she is aware that it is highly impossible to catch any of them unless she develops the act of tree climbing over night. Anyway, that is her problem and I don't see why I should lose my sleep over her intentions. In my opinion she should be minding her own business and leave the poor squirrels in peace because I still think that these squirrels have the right of existence in this park. But who will explain that to Jackie? Always on his fours and the only thing that distracts her attention from the squirrels is the periodic yelling of "stop Jackie stop and leave those creatures alone and come back here now!" She obliges but soon back to action. Talk of the right of existence! What about that small bundle of wool called Pommi or whatever his owner calls him? He thinks no one has the right to walk along his fenced yard without his permission. Whenever I walk pass his fence on my way to the park he runs along the fence barking at me until I am out of his sight, for no reason whatsoever. I am sure he misbehaves to anyone taking that route pass his yard. Luckily, he is fenced into the yard. I hope there is no chance of him getting out of the fence. What a small brat with such incredibly loud vocal sound! He does not even obey his owner's call to calm down. As long as the assumed intruder is within his sight, he would keep barking. Unfortunately, there is no other alternative route for me to the park, so I have to put up with his nuisance, and get used to it. Sometimes I wonder why and how I attract the hostile attention of these tiny little ones. Maybe I am an imaginary threat to them. I always wish they get to understand what a gentle giant I am and not assume immediate threat and danger at the sight of me. My sonny was the only one who felt safe, at home and comfortable with me even at the very first time we met. He was teasingly bold with me without any inhibitions. His initial approach to me was astonishing but I took a sincere liking to him, in a way that I never felt before. He is always very sincere and says things as he sees it. I really miss him now. Hope he will be back soon and I am sure he will have lots of story to tell about the competition. Even the very thought of him kept me awake here in the park otherwise I would have slept off on this bench. Got to go now. I know that Mrs. Jones must be waiting for our regular walk around our neighbourhood. Unfortunately, she does not like sitting here in the park, not even when Mr. Jones was with us. She prefers meeting and chatting with our neighbours and acquaintances to sitting idly on this bench. It is an honour to be with and assist her around.

Today I have a feeling that Carl is in the park. I can pick his scent from home and I can't wait get to the park as soon as I can. I am sure he will be eager to see me as well.

"Hey grandpa, what are you doing here? I did not see you dosing on your bench when I entered the park. Usually I spot you as soon as I enter the park but I could hear you snoring even before I approached the gate. Today I was surprised you were not there when I came in. I am even more surprised to see you down here at this far end of the park. Are you sure you haven't lost your way, your memory or anything? I can lead you to your bench and return here to play with my mates. You look tired and added some weight. Are you ok grandpa?

"Carl, I am fine and have not lost my way. When I got ready to come to the park I could pick up…"

"Wait a minute grandpa, I think I know where you are trying to tell me. I know it, I know it. The next thing I have to hear is that you picked up my scent far away from the park. I don't think that I have a scent. What is my scent like?"

"Carl, you have not allowed me to talk and explain things to you yet. We all have our scent that in unique to us as individuals. But indeed, you are very smart. You were able to read my mind and predict accurately what I was about to say. Yes, I picked up your scent from home that lead me straight to where you are now. I could not resist coming down here because your scent was getting stronger and stronger as I was closing up on you."

"Ok grandpa, I agree with you but first tell me what my scent is like and how it is different from others. I fart sometimes and I know it smells different from that of Princess and Budo but I did not fart today. When I do, I make sure no one around hears the sound but all will share in the flavour equally, unlike Budo. One thing with Budo is that he likes to celebrate his fart. First he stands up from his usual lying down position, shakes his hind legs a couple of times and then let go. It sounds like Mr. Smith just switching on his car ignition which unfortunately is not the best sound in the neighbourhood. After that he walks around the house to make sure that none of the products is wasted. As for Princess, she is so secretive farting. So, tell me what my scent is like."

"It is hard to explain Carl, and has nothing to do with you farting or not, but as soon as you entered the park I picked it up from my home to where we are now. Trust me on that Carl. Now about the competition, how did it go? I am sure you performed very well because you trained very hard for it."

"Grandpa I notice that you have added a lot of weight and the deep wrinkles on your face are almost overlapping each other and those long flapping ears look very full and shinning. I wish I could grow mine like that someday. They are really gorgeous. Do they come in the way when you are eating?"

"Carl, I have already mentioned to you that your ears will never grow any longer than they are now. Not at all. I wish they could because you truly want them to. As for mine I wouldn't say that they interfere in any way with my activities because I had them this long from the time I was born, I believe."

"Grandpa, look, look, look over there. There goes Cosper. Watch what he is going to do. He is very nice, gentle and friendly. He will always poop at that same spot on daily bases. After that, all he does is to scrape the soil by kicking backwards with his back legs a couple of times. We all do that, don't you grandpa? You know what I mean. By doing so he gladly walks away hoping that he successfully covered and concealed his poops with soil. Again, we all assume the same way."

"Do you mean to tell me that nobody picks after him Carl? Does he have an owner?"

"Of course he does have an owner grandpa. That young teenage girl sitting there is the owner but she hardly takes her eyes off her book to care for what Cosper does in the park. Even when she sees him do his thing she simply ignores."

"I see. That is not Cooper's fault because he cannot clean after himself. We all cannot. We rely on the humans to do that job for which we are grateful."

"Ok grandpa, try to get this right. His name is Cosper. Cos, Cos, Cos. Not Cooper. Cooper is a different playmate of mine who does not misbehave that way or should I say has a more responsible owner. There are a couple of cases where the owners do not pick the poops. Every now and then you come across poops littered all over the place in this park. I don't blame you for not being aware of this fact because you simply lump down on that bench and doze off. And I am sure no one will be bold enough to poop around you. I would be scared to do so."

"Cosper's, did I get the name right this time Carl? Cosper's owner should be advised by the park manager, of the need for her to pick after Cosper in order to maintain the cleanliness on this park. Don't you think so? I am going back to my bench. Talk to you later Carl."

"See you later grandpa."

"It's nice to see you after such a long time, Carl. But remember, I am eager to hear all about your performance at the competition. I am sure you did very well."

CHAPTER TEN

CARL DOES NOT SOUND very happy to me and it seems very unwilling to discuss the show competition. Something must have gone wrong somewhere, somehow. I hope Princess did not give him hard time at the competition. I will find out when he joins me but for now let me go and take a nap on my bench. This part of the park has really changed quite a lot from what I could remember of it. On that fateful day Mr. Jones strolled me as usual in a baby pram into the park to our usual bench. I never saw him dose off while still holding his newspaper or whatever he called it. He will always say "Sonny my newspaper" and I am at the door to bring it in as soon as the gentleman drops it by our doorway and drops it by his table side. And as he gets ready to come to the park I was always excited to pick it up again and hop into the pram. That used to be my daily routine and nothing excites me more than that. And so, when I saw him dose off he was really into it, tired after all-day long working in his garden. Out of curiosity I decided to explore the rest of the park. Slow and steadily I drifted down the gentle slope towards the sandy lake. I saw many anxious faces gazing at me for reasons I did not understand, That, made me very uncomfortable but I kept moving down the slope not knowing what to expect. As soon as I hit the sand I became more and started hopping and skipping uncontrollable. I got some one more excited and heard the most blood chilling barking of my life that hunts me to date. This huge fellow charged at me and all I instinctively did was to lay down on the ground, gently turned to my side and then turned on my back with my legs up in the air in total submission. Despite the fact that he was on leash and being dragged backward by the owner he insisted that I did something very wrong for not being leashed but enjoying an unconceivable freedom happily hopping around in his territory. For that I need to be taught a bitter lesson. I could feel his deep breath on me. I felt trapped, lying on my back. All I could do was to keep turning my head in the direction of his advances. Luckily for me he was leashed but the poor tiny lady who happened to be his owner was no match to his strength. Before long the commotion attracted a huge crowd, all holding tight on to their leashes and eager to know what was going on. One of the men stepped in and lifted me up and for a moment I felt safe. As he carried me away from the noisy scene I could hear Mr. Jones shouting and calling aloud: "Blonn! Blonn! Blonn, where are you? Having recognised his voice, I felt safer and started whining. Mr. Jones approached close enough to recognise that I got myself into trouble. He wasn't too happy about it but showed profound gratitude to the gentleman carrying me in his arms. As soon as he was close to me I limped forward and he caught me. Safest in his arms I wailed non-stop until we got back to the bench.

The gentleman who later came to be called Joe became a good friend of Mr. Jones and would drop by the bench to chat with Mr. Jones daily before he passed away. Once in a while he would drop by in the park to say hi to Mrs. Jones. Later we saw less of him but I will always remember him as my saviour. That was the first and last time to date that I visited this part of the park. I must admit it has really undergone a lot of transformation, safer to all. I also acknowledge the fact that only the socialised are let off leash into this valley end of the park. The un-socialised and aggressive ones still on leash as owners are responsible for any unruly behaviours.

"Eh grandpa, why are you still lumped down here? You must have been day-dreaming all these while. I thought you are back up there to your bench. Do you like it here? But remember this part of the park is for those on their feet running wild chasing one another. But for you to try running that fast, something has to be done to take care of those massive, long ear lobes of yours. No dosing and day-dreaming takes place here. But I can help teach you how to run fast, really fast and dodge objects on your part at the same time. But trust me it takes a lot of training and constant practice to achieve that and stay safe without injuries."

"Yes I know all that, Carl, but I am not ready for that kind of physical activity. I am heading to my bench right away and hope to meet you there later."

"Bye grandpa. I like your ears and wish to grow mine too."

I can't believe that I laid on this ground for such a long time just living in the past and not knowing that I was not seated on my bench. I really got carried away without realising how noisy it is down here. But think of it, with all the noise and running around which I was not mindful of, everyone is happy and feels safe and secured here. This is in direct contrast to the past here. On the other hand, having to deal with many, means that the ones like Cooper, no Casper or whatever his name is, will poop unnoticed and simply walk away without the owners picking after them. The park will be unattractive with unpicked poops lying here and there. Right up there to my bench such things do not happen. Wait a minute, I can see someone seated on my bench. So, odd. It never happened before that someone occupied my spot on the bench. How do I deal with that situation, now? But I don't have to lose my spot to them now otherwise it will be lost forever. There, he is leaving and the little one with him is not so happy. Don't tell me that, that is Pommi. Yes, the notorious Pommi. Again, he is turning and barking at me. May be that's why the owner is leaving. I guess I am a bit intimidating to him. Glad they, or rather the owner has decided to leave. But Pommi is not prepared to back out. He is still barking at me, demanding freedom to show off his powers. Little wonder he is on leash which again I never observed in this park in the recent past. But why should that bother me? I love peace and I hate violence of any kind. I will be interacting with him on my way to and from the park and as such I have to get used to it. Oh! There comes Carl.

"Hey Carl what's on with you? You look tired and worn out. Are you feeling ok? Come and tell me all about the competition."

"Everything went well but our team did not win in our most favourite events."

"Now Carl, what team are you talking about? Do you mean to say that Carl did not win? I can understand that but with the team thing I get confused."

"Grandpa, sometimes I wonder what life was like when you were young like me with no parks and good friends to play with. Always on leash both outside and inside the homes too. Sniffing, barking and fighting each other for no good reasons. Things have changed a lot now for the better compared to your good old days, if ever there was really anything good then."

"Carl, you are always right, now about the competition and the TEAM! To begin with, Carl what is this team deal that is more important to you than you as an individual?"

"I admire your wisdom a lot and your eagerness to catch up with the present but I don't really know where and how to start explaining things to you, grandpa. But if you will concentrate and pay attention I shall explain the events in detail. Some of the events, I am sure will fall above your level of comprehension but I do understand. Just pay attention as much as possible and everything will be fine."

"Ok Carl enough of all these! I am fully attentive to you now. Come up with it and explain the events and the team. I am all ears."

"Yes grandpa, I can see those ears for myself but I like them. It goes like this. Pay attention! Every event has the Individual event and the Team event. In the Individual events participants, can compete in any event that they feel comfortable in if they qualify. Tell me when you are not following so I can simplify the terms. I mean the terms and not the teams, ok? Your chances of winning depends on how hard you trained as well as how good you are at the event. In the Team events, it is the collective efforts of the team members that determines the success or failure of the team in that event. But to be selected as a team member is highly competitive but to qualify in the individual events is a bigger challenge. Usually all the team members are not equally well trained for the event."

"I understand that, Carl. Let's come back to the main point and discus the competition."

"Be patient grandpa. I know that you are eager to hear about the events and I am coming to that. I participated in the competition on both the individual and team events. I really trained very hard daily in this park. You saw me running very fast all over the place. Actually, I am the fastest in this park. Whenever I stand to compete in any events the humans will be shouting "Go Carl Go! Go Carl Go!! Go Carl Go!!! They crowd loves me because they know that I am the best and will always win. I feel very happy and ready for action when I hear them screaming and praising me before the event. I always win and make them even more proud of me. The last thing I can think of is to disappoint the crowd."

"You told me that before Carl, and I am also a good fan of yours and I want to see you win. Can we now talk about the team event?"

"In the team event grandpa, the picture is different because a lot of things influence the success or failure each time. Each team comprising of participants in a common event or events take up a name. For example, there is one called the UP JOHN. A very lousy team made up of spoilt brats from rich owners. They are not trained in anything and never qualifies for the final events but are only known to display the most expensive costumes. There is the GO GETTER team. Nice and highly competitive team. The PUSH OVERS are highly talented and motivated but are never organised and lack effective leadership. Every one of the team is highly trained but wants to dominate the rest. We are known as the JONES PARK Team. Grandpa, there are a couple more teams that take part in the competition but these four teams are the most popular for various reasons. Among these four teams the JONES PARK team has all the best qualities rolled up in one. We are the favourite with the crowd. We all belong to this park and you know how well behaved and serious we take our training. Above all the JONES PARK team is the only team that enjoy the benefit of an off-leash park facilities. I was often told that this is the closest and only off-leash park around."

"Hold on Carl please. Do you mean to say that this park is known as the JONES PARK?

"NO grandpa it is just the name given to the team that trains in this park. That's why I told you to listen carefully and concentrate in what I am trying to tell you about the competition. Anyway Mr. Smith is on his way up to pick me. Nice talking to you. By the way you are getting smarter and catching up remarkably well. Talk to you later and goodbye"

"Goodbye Carl"

CHAPTER ELEVEN

MEETING WITH CARL YESTERDAY was indeed very remarkable even though I did not satisfy my curiosity regarding his achievement at the competition. My inner feelings tell me that Carl did not fare well as he expected. That is more than enough to devastate him because he worked or rather trained very hard preparing for the competition. I am sure that if that is the case I would be equally devastated since the last thing that I could bare is to see him sad and disappointed for any reason. He spoke about team event in which case his success in the event will depend on the collective efforts by his team mates the way I understand him and not just by his effort alone. He never mentioned about his team and his team members who happen to belong to this park. Yes, the JONES PARK TEAM. Come to think of it. Could that be a coincidence linking Mr. Jones to this park long after his death. But I have no clue at all that this park is named after Mr. Jones. Could be a coincidence. I recall that he was one of the first users from the very beginning of the park. I also recall that before development started in the park Mr. Jones strolled me in the baby pram pass this area with no activities inside. I recall also that when development started later he would stroll me in and would spend most of the time talking with the developers. He never missed a day not being in the park. Sometimes, they would be waiting on him to step into the park and as soon as they spotted him they would not let go of him until late in the day. He appeared to be very indispensable to the developers in whatever they were doing. I recall also that for a very long time the person I spent most of the time in the park was Mrs. Jones. Come to think of it. The JONES PARK team. The fact that no one ever occupies this bench except Mrs. Jones and Blonn. Later on, now only Blonn occupies the bench. Did Mr. Jones own the park and gifted it to the public. He was that generous, I know. I would not be surprised if that was the case and if that is the case, I got the clue from my association with Carl. I am sure that Mrs. Jones would not like to bother me with that information. Of what importance, would that information be to Blonn? she would think. And she is right. I would rather not ask her about it, hereafter. My gratitude to Carl and I am highly indebted to him. I am really catching up with time because of him. I have learnt a lot from him already I must admit. Oh! There he comes.

"Carl, I have not seen you for such a long time and you look very much upset now. What is the matter with you.? Who is troubling you now and how can I help?"

"Grandpa we met not long ago, have you forgotten? I need your advice now. The groomer is changing her ways with us now and it is making me nervous. She is becoming too familiar with the three of us including Mr. Smith and I don't like how things are going on at home, these days."

"What Carl, are you talking about? If she is getting familiar with all, that means she in getting to know and like you better. You don't have to be afraid of her anymore and she will likely treat you better in her salon, hereafter. Don't you think so, Carl?"

"Grandpa you don't seem to understand the situation very well. She is getting even more familiar with Mr. Smith and he keeps on talking endlessly with her, laughing and chatting for what I do not know. Whenever he comes to the saloon to pick us up after grooming he ignores our presence as soon as she starts her conversation. That's when I hate her the most. As for Mr. Smith, I cannot begin to tell you how much he enjoys the situation while we on our part, are longing to leave the saloon. The sooner the better. But unfortunately, Mr. Smith tend to disregard our body language in her presence. That's when I come to the rescue of Budo, Princess and myself. You know how, and it really works."

"Come on Carl, they are humans. They have to interact with one another from time to time. I know you are tired after grooming but try to understand and do not hate her more for that reason. It does not happen very often."

"Grandpa, follow what I am trying to explain to you and then advise me. It is happening more often than the usual and I am beginning to feel somehow. You know, grandpa Mr. Smith usually brings me to this park, watches and cheers me up while I practice and later takes me home. He was always there for me and I liked it. These days, he brings me here and as soon as I begin my training practices he sneaks out only sneak in again just before we head home. I notice his absence and keep wondering where he goes when he goes away. Strange isn't it grandpa?"

"Carl, I think he is busy with something and as soon as that is over he will be his usual self. Humans are always like that. So, let's talk about your events at the competition. How many prizes did you win?"

"You know what, grandpa, Mr. Smith is getting more and more distracted away from us even at home. A couple of times he forgot to feed us. Budo was so hunger that he would have severed and eaten up my tail if I wasn't very careful. At another time, he fed us and slept off without taking Budo and I out to poop. As a result, Budo pooped all over the house when he could no longer hold up."

"That's funny and serious as well Carl. I truly agree with you and I think something serious is happening to him."

"No grandpa that is not funny. What is funny is that you think it is funny. How can that be? You are blessed with lots of wisdom and very old enough to come up with better ideas than I am able to. Do you know what, grandpa? Last time I observed the groomer lady talking with Mr. Smith just outside our home for a very long time instead of playing with us inside the house as usual. I was not happy to see her near our home talking to Mr. Smith. I don't enjoy that happening in her saloon after grooming but for that to occur near our home nearly blew my head off."

"Now we are getting at something, Carl"

"Getting at what grandpa? Last time after I left the park with Mr. Smith the lady was at the entrance to the park. As soon as she saw us she joined us. On the way, home both of them were talking and laughing. I wasn't happy at all to say the least. Finally, we parted ways and she left as soon as we reached home. Just now before coming to the park she entered our house for the very first time. I was in shock and before I knew what I was doing I was growling at her with my teeth clenched but tightly closed. She could see that I wasn't very pleased to meet her and all she could alter was 'Hey Carl. It's me Tina. Don't you remember?" With a wave of hand, she beckoned on me to come and say hello to her. I stopped growling when Mr. Smith shouted from somewhere. 'stop Carl stop'. Budo rushed expectantly to her thinking that she was handing out a treat to me. Princess was seated on her high perch observing situations. As for me I would want to severe those fingers off her hand."

"Carl hold it there. We have now landed."

"Oh no grandpa. What are you talking about.? I was telling you how Mr. Smith has changed or changing these days and you are talking of landing. I understand how you can drift easily into day dreaming from time to time on minor thoughts but to, day dream of flying and landing is something serious. Are you at all with me all along?"

"No Carl, I am not day dreaming and I am fully present, alert and I am with you. What I mean to say is that based on my experience in life so far I think I understand what is going on between Mr. Smith and the groomer lady. Did I hear you call her Tina? Yes, Tina and Mr. Smith are hooking up together."

"Hooking up! What does that mean? Can you explain what hooking up means in a way that the very young like me could understand. Your generation are used to very old ideas that we the younger generation, used to new and modern terms, do not understand."

"My generation will say it as it is. For that we would say that they are planning to live together and get married later. Carl, that means..."

"Hold on grandpa, did I hear you say live together and get married? Don't even think of it. Wait Mr. Smith and the groomer lady will live together and get married."

"Carl, I am not arranging it for them but based on all I heard from you I am beginning to think that they are heading in that direction because they love each other and if that is what Mr. Smith wants we have to encourage and support their intentions in our best interest."

"Encourage and support their what? I can't believe that I am hearing these words from you. Get married? Live in the same house. Grandpa, please give me a good shake-up and wake me up from this dream. Is that what day dreaming looks like? No that can't happen. Mr. Smith, Princess, Budo, Tina or whatever she calls herself and Carl living together in the same house as what and for how long?"

"Carl I know exactly how you feeling now. I felt the same way when Mrs. Jones joined Mr. Jones and I before he died. But we finally achieved great understanding and happiness living together. Right now, I cannot imagine life without Mrs. Jones even though she is sick and hate to use the word 'disabled' to describe her present condition. Take this from old grandpa, she will turn out to be everything you will ever desire, in the near future. Just give her a chance with an open mind and DO NOT HATE TINA too early, Carl."

"Grandpa I like and respect your opinion. You are blessed with great wisdom and always looking on the positive side of things. Were you always a positive thinker not believing on the negativities or did it come with old age? It will be great to swallow my pride and believe in your prediction. But remember that Mrs. Jones did not harm you before living with you and Mr. Jones, did she?"

"No she did not but just like you, I felt insecure initially thinking that I would lose him to her. But that did not happen. We got along well very shortly. All my ancestors are known to love peace and were looked upon as gentle giants. But Carl you can develop the same attitude by exaggerating the good qualities and diminishing the bad qualities in others. Make it a part of your life and you will be happy you did. No enemies and hatred. Replace those with love and friendship."

"Thank you grandpa for the advice. That means I will no longer skip pooping on the grooming day and I believe, you know what that means. And what will I do then when she pulls and tugs on my hair while on her grooming table? No grandpa

I don't believe Mr. Smith will do that to us. You are the wisest but I think you are wrong this time. I cannot see it happening."

"Carl how is Princess getting along with you?"

"Oh she is the best and you know what she did during the competition? Eh! Hold on grandpa. We are discussing how to help Mr. Smith change his strange behaviour. Stay focused on that for now and later I will tell you all about the competition."

"I am glad you have not forgotten about the competition and from what I gathered from you, now, Princess is now nice to you Carl, because you were finally patient and willing to give her the chance to do so. Am I, right? Eh Carl, look at that."

"Grandpa, her name is Pooly. Doesn't she look very gorgeous? She was there at the salon also."

"Oh yes Carl. She is very nice. I saw her enter the park sometime back and quickly acknowledged to myself how nice she looked. The groomer did a very good styling on her and I like the way she carries herself. A very elegant and graceful way of walking. How did Pooly behave at the salon, Carl?"

"Very well behaved, grandpa. She was being groomed when we entered. There was no form of protest from her even when her hair was being tugged and pulled on while being groomed. From the inside of my cage I could make out from her reaction that she was not enjoying the process but never complained. Above all she was very obedient and was the darling of the groomer. At the end, she gracefully hopped down from the table with the expression of peace, joy and happiness radiating from her face. What a gentle giant, grandpa. She likes to socialize with everyone and we all like her a lot. Whenever she approaches an angry one as she usually does the situation changes from barking to occasional whining. But as soon as she leaves the salon the pent-up anger erupts and noisy aftermath is unbearable. Something in her is unique not forgetting the spotless white, amazing coat. She is a clean freak. You never see her rolling on the ground like I do sometimes. I admire her a lot grandpa."

"She is really and the lady accompanying her into the park is equally elegant. There seems to be a very cordial relationship between the two of them. Do you agree with me, Carl?"

"Oh yes Grandpa she was there at the competition. She won the top prize in the dancing competition. Everybody loved her. She danced with a very nice lady, her owner, and both of them displayed very intricate movements on stage. To watch her standing on her back legs, both arms in the air, taking foot-steps, sideways, front and back in tune with the music is very amazing. I really loved and enjoyed her talents. I am sure you have never seen anything like that before especially her dancing talents."

"Carl I am sure that if you are impressed with her performance the way you put it, she must be very good at dancing or whatever that means to us. But what I don't understand is why she is the way he looks. Interesting but at the same time "funny. She wasn't born that way, I believe."

"No grandpa, she comes to the groomer too. I mean that lady, Tina or whatever she calls herself. At one time, she was on the grooming able before we walked in, one day. As usual, Tina was tugging and pulling at Pooly's hair so much that I could feel the pain and agony she was undergoing. I nearly threw up watching her endurance. Pooly did not complain. She displayed happy disposition all through the grooming and when it was all done released she sprinted gracefully down from the table wagging his tail from side to side happily. At the competition Pooly has a very dignified way of walking. She takes very graceful steps and interacts with people with such self-confidence that everybody loved to pet her. Above all, she seems to love and cherish the attention he attracted to herself."

"I see what you mean Carl. I love the way she carries herself as well as her happy dispositions, but I still wonder whose idea it was to groom her that way."

"Grandpa it was all Tina's ideas. Who else will it be? You should have seen Pooly on the grooming table after being washed, blow-dried and fluffed up. She looked the best that way in my opinion, until that Tina decided to play the havoc on the beautiful snow-white hairs with her grooming tools. On the dancing stage Pooly looked good in that hair-cut. I admired her hopping and flipping around the stage with her lady-owner. Even now I admire her a lot but we must stop Tina before she hits on Mr. Smith. Please grandpa we must do something immediately."

"So, Carl do you mean to say that she was full haired when you saw her at the groomer?"

"Yes grandpa she was and really full all over. Not part shaved here and there the way he looked now. In no time her hairs will definitely grow back to be full."

"Her owner must have requested Tina to groom him this way.

In that case, Tina is not to blame. But I tell you something Carl, a couple of times, I see one of us enter this park regularly. He is much smaller than Pooly but a little more unpleasant looking. With long straight hairs on his feet, tip of his tail, on top of his head and running down to the tip of his tail. Hard to maintain steady eye contact with him for long. Very scary to look at."

"That is Crestie, grandpa. He is very friendly. He does not bond easily with anyone as he spends a long-time mind-reading.

At first, he could not befriend me easily because he hates to run around in the park like I do. But now he cannot stay away from me in this park for too long. He comes running to me as soon as he sees me. He also took part in the agility event of the competition."

"Now Carl, don't tell me he has anything to do with Tina because I have been seeing him in this park much earlier than I met you. I can assure you that he was never full haired. But, why is his skin so patched up. Poor thing! He must have been badly burnt by fire judging from the look of his skin. Lucky, he survived. Thanks to that veterinarian who treated him."

"Yes grandpa, Crestie I am sure was born that way. He was never burnt by fire and that wicked veterinarian did not treat him of burnt. Do not praise him for doing nothing. I have never seen him in full hair at anytime. Luckily for him, he has nothing to do with Tina and her salon."

"In that case Carl, would you want to look like him and never having to go to the groomer? I am sure you would not for any reason like to be born that way. Very soon you will come to tolerate Tina and most likely be friends with her in the near future if you agree to give her a fair chance to study each other. Remark my words, good things will result in association with Tina."

"I agree with you grandpa if you think that Mr. Smith will change for the better. But what happens if he does not change?"

"Carl remember when you were not happy with Princess and you wanted to…"

"Yes grandpa, I remember requesting you to take her away to another because she has very irritating behaviour and does annoying things in the house but now she has changed a lot. She behaves excellent, very loving and caring. In fact, Budo and I are jealous of each other vying for her affection. That's another issue because Budo is getting on my nerves now."

"In what way Carl?"

"Grandpa, remember that Princess enjoys a tastier feed than what Budo and I have. Princess is aware of that and because of that she always leaves some feed I her plate for us. Budo, being greedy wallops his feed quickly and waits on Princess to back off. I am sure he does not chew up before swallowing. But Princess is very smart. She will guard her plate and the left over until I finish my portion. As soon as she backs off Budo will dive, towards her plate and wallops whatever is left there too."

"Carl, I am sure you can run faster than Budo and should be able to reach the plate before him. Perhaps you spend too much time on your plate."

"Of course I can run much faster than Budo. In fact, he cannot run at all. But grandpa that's not the point. It has nothing to do with speed. Budo is too fat, you know. We get to her plate almost at the same time but I get knocked over by him, each time. If you and I are to rush off for some tasty treat very close-by, you will definitely knock me over because you are much, much fatter than I am and have the weight advantage. But if the treat is far away and we are to run for it, I have many advantages over you because I run faster, I am much younger, I am not fat at all and my ears will not be a problem. In fact, I will reach the treat, finish it and rest well before you arrive. Do you get my problem with Budo?"

"Carl, I am not fat. I am big with very lean muscles. Don't be surprised if I out run you because of my long legs.

I am happy that you appreciate Princess and that she is good to you. As for Budo we shall find a way to patch up things between both of you. He is a very good friend of yours except where feed is concerned. That's an issue to bother about. I shall help you solve that problem. With regard to Mr. Smith, humans are smarter than we are and will always take care of situations in the good interest of the family including us. So, don't worry Carl, he will be just fine."

"Outrun me? Oh, no grandpa! You have never seen me in action. There comes Mr. Smith to pick me up. Can you see them holding hands, talking and laughing? I find it hard to tolerate this behaviour. Talk to you again grandpa. Bye!"

"Bye Carl. You will be fine. See you soon."

CHAPTER TWELVE

POOR CARL! HE SEEMS to be having too much to worry about. I hate to see him upset. How I wish I would be able to help him. I realise he is just a growing kid having to face the ever-changing world around him. He seems to be taking things too seriously and my objective will be to make him see things in a mature way. By doing so I hope I will not be pushing him too far into seeing things in a more matured manner rather than allow him make mistakes and learn through such mistakes. But as long as he is open to discuss issues with me I believe he has a lot of confidence in me. The last thing I would allow myself do is to disappoint him in any way. I understand that I need a lot of patience while dealing with him. For instance, it's been long since he got back from the competition but even though I genuinely want to hear all about the events at the competition, all I could gather so far is about the different teams at the competition and what each of the teams is popular for in the eyes of the fans. The UP

JOHNS, the GO GETTERS, the PUSH OVERS and finally the JONES PARK TEAM which is currently plaguing my curiosity. Of course, he did mention that his team, the JONES PARK did not finish well in their favorite events. On individual level, he has only mentioned about the dancing Pooly and Crestie the agility event. So far he has not told me about his individual participation. Like I said before I have to be patient with him. The most pressing need for me now is to solve his issue with his housemate and friend, Budo. As far as Tina's issue is concerned Carl has to be open minded, flexible, compassionate and patient to allow things work out the way Mr. Smith designed it to be. If things are the way I imagine it to be and Mr. Smith transforms Tina to Mrs. Smith, then Carl has no other choice but to welcome the change and adapt with the reality as early as possible or risk bitter response from Mr. and Mrs. Smith. Moreover, this is not the right time for him to lose his friendship with Budo over struggle for left-over feed in the house. I feel this will be too much issues to be handled by such a young growing mind such as Carl. He is very smart and I am sure he will handle the situation by himself with a little bit of guidance which is where I come in. I must act fast before he earns bad opinion from Tina. There he comes. He does not look upset. Let me see what he is up to.

"Hey Carl, you look very cheerful and I am happy for you. What is going on with … Wow! You stink awful. Did you have an encounter with that little thing by your fence?"

"With what, grandpa? Don't tell me you are up again with your claims of scent picking."

112

"Carl if that is what I mean by picking up scent from far then it is not a gift from nature. This is different and anyone can detect this peculiar stink from you. Moreover, anyone familiar with this peculiar odour will know what was responsible for it.

Now tell me Carl, who won the encounter? You or the little creature?

"Ok, grandpa you seem to know what truly happened. I was at the yard minding my own business. Budo was also with  me when that creature sneaked in through the fence. At first I tried to frighten and chase it away. Budo normally pays least attention to this type of situation but this time he was more than anxious to end that menace. That creature ducked away but returned to challenge me. Can you imagine the boldness for it to enter our fenced yard, uninvited? I charged at it once again but as I closed on it, it simply turned around and let out the worst gas from its tunnel. It was like cloud, moist, painful and nearly blinded me. Have you ever experienced it at any time?"

"I have not, Carl. When I was your age, I was always curious to play with it because the creature you are talking about looks very clean and attractive. But I also remember Mr. Jones shouting 'Skunk! Skunk!! Blonn stay away from that creature. It is not fun to play with. You will get sprayed, so stay away from it'. I always obeyed his instructions. I usually like to admire that creature from a great distance whenever I see it. Skunks appear peaceful and tend to mind their way. But if you seek their trouble they are ready to defend themselves. That's how they fight back. Unfortunately, you are not aware of it but the smell from the spray will be there for a long time no matter how you try to wash it off from your body, Carl."

"Grandpa, you are not helping now. I am sure when I dive into that lake for a swim the smell will vanish. One of the participants at the competition had similar odour and it was very strong. Much stronger than mine. I had to avoid him for the rest of the competition. But …"

"Wait Carl. Hold it there for now. What competition are you referring to?"

"Grandpa, there you go again. How come you forget things so fast. Yes, you are very old but at the same time very wise, smart and intelligent. Those are the qualities I look forward to, when I grow old. But when it comes to forgetting faster than I learn, I do not wish to grow old at all. Recently our show was held and in that, some competition events in which I was part of were conducted. Did you remember that I was away for a long while?"

"Oh, yes Carl, of course I remember you not seen in this park for a long time. But there is something that I am trying hard not to forget."

"What is it grandpa? I can teach you how not to forget things at all. That's how I remember everything. It is easy, if you allow me to be the young teacher and you not too young student."

"Ok, Carl, someone told me about the UP-JOHNTEAM, the PUSH OVERTEAM, the

GO GETTER TEAM and finally the last one I have forgotten. I cannot remember the last the name but it ended with Park team"

"Grandpa are you talking about the JONES PARKTEAM? That is my home …wait a minute grandpa, how do you know about the teams at the competition? I am sure you were not there at the event and don't try to convince me that you can also pick up sound, just like you pick up scent from far. I will find it hard to believe."

"That's funny Carl. I am the one to teach you how to remember things easily starting from now. I did not forget hearing about those teams from Carl, but the same Carl did not remember telling me about the teams. Now which is better? To be old but act young or to be young but…? I have been waiting to hear all the details about the events and how you fared in it. I knew you will somehow remember to tell grandpa all about the events."

"Did I? I must have told you all that happened at the competition events. Try harder to remember, grandpa."

"The last thing you told me was how Pooly and his owner danced very well at the dancing competition, displaying those intricate movements. Nothing much about Carl and Jones Park Team. But I am sure you still have so much to tell me about the event."

"Grandpa, you are a genius. You are more intelligent and smarter than I can imagine. How did your generation entertain the humans, when the idea of competition event did not exist? Probably by barking and fighting among yourselves."

"The humans entertained us instead. They brought us to the parks to watch their children play and perform plays on the stage inside the parks. Carl, it was interesting then as long as we remained by their sides all through."

"On leash! grandpa, All the time!! How can you claim it was interesting when you were not allowed to run around freely in the park, as we do now? I prefer playing off-leash to playing on-leash at any cost."

"I agree with you Carl. You are right. Better off-leash than on-leash. Mr. Smith will soon be around to pick you home. When we meet next time, I look forward to hearing all about the competition. I will remind you of it, Carl. I do not know when or how soon that would because the weather is changing fast. Very soon we will not be visiting the park for a long time."

"What are you talking about grandpa? The park will always be open… Oh no, wait now I remember. The park looks nice and green all over but may later turn white and cold. It happened then and I did not like it. Are you telling me it will happen again, grandpa? Please tell me it will not."

"I wish I could do something to prevent it from happening again. But unfortunately, it will surely happen again, again and again. I have seen it happen many times. I can understand how you are feeling because that memory will always be alive. The first time, Mr. Jones brought me to the park cradled in his big arms, he would let me hop around under his watchful supervision. As soon as he sensed danger, he would grab and hold onto me for a while and then let go of me. I enjoyed myself then but slowly and gradually, we stopped coming to the park. I remember him reminding me saying 'Blonn soon it will be bitterly cold, the leaves will drop off the trees and the green grass here in the park will be covered in snow. When that time comes, we would stop coming to the park. I don't like that happening but I promise you that later the snow will clear and the grass will grow back even better and we would return to the park'. Just like you are now, I was confused and did not like the idea at all. But I have experienced it happen many times. So, even though this type of change will never stop I promise you that you will soon return to play in the park as usual afterwards."

"But grandpa, how can you say that it will happen again when I still feel warm after running around? I do not feel any changes in or around me and I am sure it will continue that way. You know that there are times, like now, when I wish I could feel cool like you do without this thick coat around me. You must be feeling very comfortable with no hairs on your body."

"Not for long Carl, you will feel better than I do now. When that change occurs, your coat will protect you better from cold. But that doesn't mean you will be out playing in this park. I know that you have had your first experience of this type of change but you were too young then to understand what was happening. As these changes happen, you will get used to it."

"Ok grandpa when will the change start? You are frightening me. I cannot think of not coming to the park at all, any day. What will I be doing at home? Just sit and gaze at Princess and Budo all day long. Tina has also joined."

"Carl, so Tina has moved in with you. Lucky for you. How is she getting along with all of you?"

"She is ok to us but we are missing Mr. Smith a lot. He does not spend as much time with us as he used to before Tina joined us. The only communication with us now is 'Princes, Carl and Buno, breakfast time. After that it is Carl and Buno it's poo time."

"What happens next, Carl?"

"After that nothings happens. He goes in and takes her to the salon. Both of them returns him late at night on their fours. Grandpa we must do something to help Mr. Smith out."

"What do you mean 'on their fours' Carl?"

"Yes, they will be talking, laughing, falling down and getting up. When they fall to the floor, they will be crawling towards any furniture for support to stand up. Last time Tina fell over a nice piece of glass mantle and it broke into tiny pieces. Mr. Smith stepped onto a tiny glass piece. He was crying like a baby because of pain. Grandpa a lot of things have changed in my home after Tina moved in. some of the changes are good but most and not too good."

"Ok Carl, I have heard enough of the 'not so good'. Time to hear of the good part of the story. Go ahead and tell grandpa. This time, we are not going to forget just as we did for the event competition. So, what are the good sides?"

"You know grandpa, Tina cooks very well and we all like her for that. She makes very tasty cookies. She offered us a little bit of the human food and it tastes really delicious. She even offered us what she calls chicken, fish, bones to chew and cookies. Little of each even when we desired more."

"You see Carl, you are beginning to like Tina but I am sure she will reveal the better side of her as time goes. All you need is the patience at f this early stage. That reminds me of the cookies you promised me of, the first time we met. Have you forgotten? You thought that I was about to cry when I remembered Mr. Jones. You said 'Don't cry grandpa, I shall bring to you a cookie next time'. I thought it was very thoughtful of you to say that, and I admired you for that."

"Grandpa, that was not a tasty cookie, was it? Wait until you taste Tina's cookie."

"Still on cookies, Carl even though you promised the cookies you forgot to deliver on it. But that's not the point. The point is that you are very thoughtful and compassionate by nature. One good thing worth mentioning is that Tina has at least one good thing about her which you like and she will continue to build on it. Believe me you will soon observe many good qualities that will draw all of you towards her,"

"Grandpa you are right. Buno is so drawn to Tina these days that he literally follows her around the house all the time. She keeps throwing tasty cookies to him. Buno has gained so much weight since Tina moved in with us that he barely stands on his fours for long without lying on his tummy. Now he cannot stand on three legs to pee. You know what I mean grandpa unless you have the same problem. As for me I can not only stand on three legs when I pee but can hop around on three for a distance. Budo feels jealous of me when I do so because he cannot attempt it anymore."

"What about Princess and you, Carl."

"Tina is very kind to us as well and we enjoy her cookies very much. The cookies are really tasty and I can pick up the flavour from here now. It makes me salivate but we are missing the company of Mr. Smith very much. Buno, on the other hand, misses him too but where food is concerned he has no compromise."

"What else does Tina do to help in running the home?"

"Do you know what grandpa? Our house is very clean and smells great these days after she moved in. Buno and I poo outside but Princess poos and pees in that box with the sand or whatever that is in it. The box stinks a lot when Mr. Jones fails to scoop out the urine and poo from the box. I always wondered why she does not have to do her business outside as Buno and I do especially when the house stinks of her urine and poo."

"So Tina keeps the house clean at all times. That's a very good thing about her Carl, don't you think so.?"

"I think so grandpa and I respect her for that. Early in the day she does all the cleaning and she is now taking over the task of feeding us. Right now, all that Mr. Smith does is to take us out in the morning. That too Tina is gradually showing interest in doing too. We are missing Mr. Smith when company a lot. We wish he could be a little more available to us."

"You will get over it soon and come to enjoy Tina's company as well as you do for him."

"What makes you think so Grandpa?"

"That is human nature, Carl. I went through what you are now, when Mrs. Jones moved in to live with Mr. Jones and I. Right now, I do not know what I would do without her."

"Was Mrs. Jones a groomer also? You did not tell me that, grandpa. But you do not have hairs on your body for you to feel the pain of grooming. Tina grooming me was very painful and that's why I did not like her at first."

"But now you are happy, Carl. I am happy for you too because I knew that will happen soon. No Mrs. Jones was never a groomer. What I mean to say is that when she came to live with us I thought that she would take Mr. Jones away from me. But that did not happen. Instead she liked me even more. In the same way, you will grow to like her more."

"Like her more than Mr. Jones? Grandpa that may never happen. I will never stand her grooming me. What about that?"

"Don't worry Carl, these humans think ahead of us. I am sure she would devise a way to make grooming easy on you."

"In what ways, grandpa? I still have my hairs on me."

"That will be up to Tina to decide but I am sure she will make it easier for you. You know Carl, when you leave your hairs too long before grooming it, it knots up making it harder to handle."

"Grandpa you are right. The longer I stay between grooms the more uncomfortable I tend to become. I feel itchy and can smell foul odour from within me. Hard to sleep well also then. But the moment I am groomed I feel very nice, smell fresh and sleep comfortably better. But grandpa how did you know all these especially when you do not have hairs on your body? I am always amazed at your wisdom."

"Now Carl, we are getting to know how best to make grooming less painful and more comfortable."

"But how will that happen, grandpa?"

"I am sure Tina knows better. What do you think would happen if you shorten the length of the in-between grooms? Instead of allowing your hair to grow too long she might decide to do so more frequently. By doing so you will feel more comfortable within yourself. The grooming will be less painful, instead of stocking your tunnel and opening it to release the gas in order to shorten your time on the grooming table."

"Grandpa, that worked very well. I enjoy looking at Tina's face when she had to smell the gas before it diffuses up. I always aim it when she is handling my rear end. She picks it up at maximum effect before it diffuses throughout the room. By the time Budo and Princess picks it up from the far end of the room the effect is less. Nevertheless, I acknowledge their reaction"

"That's funny Carl, but you don't have to do that any longer if she decides to groom you more frequently. Moreover Mr. Smith will not have to spend a lot to make the three of you happier."

"You may be right, grandpa but I still think grooming will always hurt me. And to do so more regularly will be most unbearable. She is always happier when I am on her table. She will be singing to herself happily while I am suffering in pain. But once I release them, you know what, grandpa you should see her face frown and the joy vanishes while mine surfaces. I like and enjoy the moment. To crown it all she is forced to set me free. "

"Carl, I should say that you are lucky to have those hairs on your body even though you hate being groomed. With the weather changes you can manage to sit here in the park much longer than I do."

"Why grandpa? You just have to sit down here without much to do. No running around chasing freebee, squirrels and dose off soundly. Those snoring actions of yours is frightening to listen to. When I hear it from that end of the park, and I do always, I tell my playmates that grandpa is at it again. That's when I come running to wake you up. What has the weather to do with…"

"You do not understand what I mean. Can you see that the leaves on the trees are beginning to change colours and falling off the branches?

"That happens all the time grandpa. Old leaves change colour and fall off because they are old. Young leaves like me keep coming up to replace them."

"You are right Carl, but that is not the case all the time. As the weather gets colder, which you have not experienced enough to understand, all the leaves will drop off gradually young and old. All, will die and fall off. The branches will remain but with on leaves on them."

"Grandpa, I do not think that will ever happen. How can we play in the park without those shades that protect us from the heat of the sun?"

"Carl the sun will not be there as it was before now. The park will be closed until the sun returns again because the weather will be very cold. It will be so cold that your coat will not keep you warm. The season is over and the park will be closed. Today, unfortunately is the last day of the season."

"But I am still warm enough if that is the problem, grandpa."

"Yes you are but the humans are like me with no thick hairs like yours to protect us from cold."

"So you are feeling cold and less comfortable now grandpa. Is that the reason you are shivering and your mouth quivering?"

"You are right Carl. I came to the park today to see you and say goodbye until we see again next summer season. But till then, remember you still have to tell me all about the competition events."

"And how long will that be before I meet you again. Promise me grandpa it will be like a couple of days and not too long."

"It won't be that too long but definitely not just a couple of days. There comes Mr. Smith and Tina to pick you up. I can see another friend of yours in their company. From your description, it looks like your good friend, Budo. Carl bye for now till we meet again. Don't worry, you have many around to keep you happy."

"Bye grandpa. I will miss you very dearly. Mrs. Jones will be there for you as well until we meet again"

END OF SEASON 1.